Barbara & Charles Middlebrook

COMPETENT TO LEAD

KENNETH O. GANGEL

MOODY PRESS
CHICAGO

Fourth Printing, 1978

ISBN: 0-8024-1608-X

Contents

Foreword

IT SEEMS to many of us that Christian leaders are, in the science of human relations, far behind our non-Christian friends who fulfill leadership roles in business, education, and the professions.

Dr. Kenneth Gangel has sought—and successfully—to correct this problem through this incisive, theologically sound, provocative book. It can well serve as a manual, guide, and textbook in the area of Christian interpersonal relationships. This is vital to successful Christian leadership, especially for the person filling a managerial role for which he feels inadequately prepared.

Leaders will be particularly impressed and helped by the strong emphasis on the effective leader's role and service. Even as our Lord "came not to be ministered unto, but to minister," so does the effective Christian executive. Dr. Gangel addresses himself to this valid and important New Testament principle and illustrates it clearly and beautifully.

This is a people-oriented book, in which Professor Gangel explores new areas of concern for the Christian leader in human relations, and provokes him to think through his role in relation to being a "laborer together." Throughout, the author indicates the kind of human relationships leaders must maintain if they are to work together harmoniously and effectively in the church and in other Christian organizations.

Much of this challenging information comprises valid and valuable science-of-management principles based upon a sound, scriptural foundation. With a great sense of balance, compassion, and concern, Dr. Gangel courageously attacks

5

some contemporary myths head-on, and offers a biblical basis
for the Christian leader's role in creating vital, interpersonal
relationships.

TED W. ENGSTROM

*To all God's people
in local churches everywhere
seeking to be "laborers together"
in the service of Christ*

For we are labourers together with God: ye are
God's husbandry, ye are God's building (1 Co 3:9).

We then as workers together with him, beseech you
also that ye receive not the grace of God in vain
(2 Co 6:1).

Introduction

IN THE LATE 1960s the institutional church was under fire from all sides. Secularists predicted its demise; renewal prophets called for radical restructuring; seminary students questioned whether they could serve within its ranks; and pastors wondered if they could continue to minister under the multiple burdens which attended their office. But the mid-1970s present a new day for the church. Enthusiasm and optimism have returned.

Meanwhile, the barbarian society continues to paganize Western culture. The salt and light of Christ's disciples were never more needed. Someone has suggested that we live in a world "come full cycle," with society's norms reflecting a greater likeness to ancient Rome than those of any intervening civilization. The need for the church's life and ministry to touch the marketplace in Athens is apparent to all who care to notice.

Yet the impact of the church upon the marketplace is still dulled by the necessity to grapple with its own problems in the sanctuary, not the least of which is the continuing Corinthian schism dividing brother from brother, group from group, and clergy from laity. The spirit of community is sacrificed on the altar of pragmatic housekeeping as we occupy ourselves with survival in the fiscal and spiritual crisis of the age.

To be very specific, many of God's people have not yet learned how to get along with each other in a fellowship of mutual service for Christ. Short tenures of pastors, directors of Christian education, and youth ministers testify to their

7

inability to win the battles of human relations, both among themselves and in the wider congregational context.

It is the purpose of this volume to speak specifically to the issue of human relations in the church and its affiliate organizations (such as schools or publishing houses). The pattern is to draw principles from both secular research and Biblical text, in an effort to blend the two into a Christian philosophy of collective service and ministry. Though many of the concepts involve an understanding of professional administration, I have tried to make them palatable for the layman. At times, therefore, the professional may detect oversimplification and overgeneralization. It seemed a reasonable price to pay in order to make this kind of information available to people who need to put it into operation in their current tasks.

1

Toward a New Testament View of Leadership

As Aesop tells the story, the frogs down on the pond wanted a king. They bothered Jupiter so much with their requests that he finally tossed a log into the pond, and for a while the frogs were happy with their new leader.

Soon, however, they discovered that they could jump up and down on the leader, run all over him, and he offered no resistance nor even a response. Not only that, but he had no direction or purpose to his behavior but just floated back and forth on the pond, a practice which exasperated the frogs, who were really sincere about wanting "strong leadership."

So back to Jupiter they went. They complained about their log leader and appealed for much stronger administrative oversight. Jupiter was weary of the complaining frogs, so this time he gave them a stork, who stood tall above the members of the group and certainly had the appearance of a leader. The frogs were quite happy with the new situation. Their leader stalked around the pond making great noises and attracting great attention. Their joy turned to sorrow, however, and ultimately to panic, for in a very short time the stork began to eat his subordinates.[1]

One of the major problems in implementing Christian leadership in the church, or in any other kind of Christian community, is failure to recognize not only a pragmatic, but also a biblical leadership style. Frequently we find ourselves gravitating to extremes and behaving like logs or storks in our relationship to the people with whom God allows us to work. The log was a "free-rein" leader, letting the followers do whatever they wanted to. The stork was at the opposite end of the continuum in his absolute autocracy.

In a *Harvard Business Review* article entitled "How to Choose a Leadership Pattern," authors Tannenbaum and Schmidt discuss the same problem with respect to secular functions of management science.

> The problem of how the modern manager can be "democratic" in his relations with subordinates and at the same time maintain the necessary authority and control in the organization for which he is responsible has come in to focus increasingly in recent years.
> Earlier in the century this problem was not so acutely felt. The successful executive was generally pictured as possessing intelligence, imagination, initiative, the capacity to make rapid (and generally wise) decisions, and the ability to inspire subordinates. People tended to think of the world as being divided into "leaders" and "followers."[2]

What is most interesting is that the leadership style which has evolved from multimillion dollars of research on the part of industrial management science is not far removed from the leadership style which Scripture delineates from the start! It is a style which recognizes the inherent value of the individual and the worth of human relations not only as a means to an end but as an end in itself within the Christian community. In a very real sense, it is correct to say that the church should be the most person-centered organization in the world. Indeed, the church which has its vertical relationships in order (theocentricity) will generally follow with proper horizontal relationships (anthrocentricity). Sometimes we get so busy "saving souls" that we forget to do anything for people. The church does not have to overemphasize the social gospel to recognize that souls are rather ethereal and invisible, but one sees people every day.

What is a biblical view of leadership? Perhaps we can best arrive at that answer by first dealing with the negative side of the question.

What New Testament Leadership Is Not

There is a marvelous passage in Luke 22 which holds some enormously valuable principles for helping us analyze our Lord's view of leadership. The passage itself is contained in verses 24 through 27, but the context is of great importance also. The Lord has just ministered to the disciples in their final supper together in the upper room. Commentators differ about whether the foot washing had taken place before the conversation or whether the conversation actually precipitated the foot washing. One thing is clear: they had just finished the bread and the cup and had experienced among themselves a worship relationship of the highest order, with the incarnate God in their midst and with the Father in heaven. It is almost unbelievable that the scene recorded in these verses could have followed that experience.

New Testament leadership is not political power-play

Immediately after sharing the symbolic representation of our Lord's flesh and blood, the disciples fell into a dispute. The word is *philoneikia* and literally means "rivalry." What is even more interesting is that this word does not describe an accidental falling into argument on occasion, but rather the possession of a habitually contentious spirit. To put it another way, because of their fondness for strife, the disciples verbally attacked one another in an attempt to gain political prominence in what they expected would be an immediately forthcoming, earthly kingdom! Martin Buber once said that persons' inability to "carry on authentic dialog with one another is the most acute symptom of the pathology of our time."

Political power-play in the church is even more reprehensible than it is in the world. Yet it is striking that even before the first church was organized at Jerusalem; before a pastor ever candidated for appointment to a congregation; before an official board ever met to design a building program, the church knew how to fight! Toward the end of the first century, John bemoaned that in one local church there was a man named Diotrephes who liked "to have the preeminence among them," and the Diotrephesian tribe has multiplied in nineteen hundred years of history.

NEW TESTAMENT LEADERSHIP IS NOT AUTHORITARIAN ATTITUDE

Luke 22:25 records our Lord's reaction to the arguments of his disciples. He offers first a comparison and then a contrast. The comparison is that their behavior at that moment was like the behavior of the Hellenistic monarchs who ruled in Egypt and Syria. Their leadership style is decribed as "exercising lordship"—the word *kurieuo,* which appears frequently in the pages of the New Testament. At times it is used to describe the authority of God (Ro 14:9). Paul uses it often to refer to a negative control, such as death's attempt to hold dominion over Christ (Ro 6:9); the power of sin in the life of the believer (Ro 6:14); and the hold of the law on men freed by the gospel (Ro 7:1).

A similar word, *katakurieuo,* is used to describe Gentile rulers; the control of demons over men (Ac 19:16); and as a negative example in prescribing the behavior of elders with saints in the church (1 Pe 5:3). The verb form is never used positively of Christian leadership. To put it very simply, *Christian leadership is not authoritarian control over the minds and behavior of other people.* Peter remembered the lesson of this night, for in writing his epistle he warned the elders not to lord it over God's heritage.

The first part of Luke 22:26 is a strong contrast construction: "But ye . . . not so." The kings of the Gentiles wished to be called benefactor for any little deed of kindness they might show to their subjects, although it was expected that they would practice autocracy and demagoguery. Whether that is right or wrong is not the issue. The point is that *Christian* leadership is *not* that kind of authoritarian control. As a matter of fact, in defiance of the culture of the time, our Lord says in this verse that the one who is greatest in the church is actually *as* the younger, and the boss is *as* the worker.

NEW TESTAMENT LEADERSHIP IS NOT CULTIC CONTROL

One of the beautiful words describing the work of the church is the word *diakanos*. It means "service" and is precisely what Christ did for his disciples in that upper room. The question of verse 27 seems to be rhetorical: Who is more important, the waiter or the dinner guest? Obvious answer: the dinner guest, of course! But wait a minute, who is the guest and who is the waiter at this Last Supper? Answer: "I am among you as he that serveth." Conclusion: *New Testament Leadership is not flashy public relations and platform personality, but humble service to the group.* The work of God is to be carried on by spiritual power not personal magnetism, as Paul clearly points out in 1 Corinthians 1:26-31. Some leaders may *serve* the Word and some leaders may *serve* tables but all leaders *serve* (Acts 6)!

THE POSITIVE PATTERN OF CHRIST

The positive pattern of Christ in developing leadership in his disciples is clearly enunciated in A. B. Bruce's helpful book, *The Training of the Twelve.*[3] He suggests that the total report of the gospels covers only thirty-three or thirty-four days of our Lord's three-and-one-half-year ministry, and John records only eighteen days. What did Christ do the rest of the time? The clear implication of the Scriptures is that He was training leaders. What kind of leaders? How did He deal with them? What were the important principles of His leadership-development program?

Although it is not the purpose of this book to deal with the total subject of leadership development, certain principles may be helpful in making a transition to a positive declaration of what New Testament leadership is.

1. The leadership of our Lord focused on individuals. His personal conversation with Peter, recorded in John 21, is a good example of the way He gave Himself to His men in an attempt to build His life and ministry into them.

2. The leadership of our Lord focused on the Scriptures. His treatment of God's absolute truth was not diluted by relativistic philosophy. It held the Old Testament in highest esteem. The rabbis had distorted God's revelation, and the Leader of leaders now came to say, "You have heard that it was said, . . . but I say to you" (Mt 5:21-48).

3. The leadership of our Lord focused on Himself. Remember, in John 14:9, how he found it necessary to say to one of the disciples, "Philip have you been so long with Me and you still have not known the Father? Take a good look at Me because if you understand Me you understand the Father" (author's paraphrase).

4. The Leadership of our Lord focused on purpose. Christ had clear-cut goals for His earthly ministry, and a limited time in which to achieve them. If you knew you had to leave your present ministry within three-and-one-half years and turn it over completely to subordinates you would be allowed to develop during that period of time, how would you go about doing it? You could do no better than follow the example of Jesus, and the result would probably be a great deal like the leadership that characterized the New Testament church.

What New Testament Leadership Is

There is a temptation, in dealing with this issue, to turn to the book of Acts because of its vivid description of early church life. Yet the book of Acts is a historical narrative, not a developed ecclesiology. We will be better helped by looking at the epistles of Paul, who apparently was commissioned by the Spirit of God to organize local churches and to describe God's plan and pattern for the functioning of those churches. Some verses in the second chapter of 1 Thessalonians will serve us well as a model.

NEW TESTAMENT CHURCH LEADERSHIP IS NURTURE

Nurture is a botanical term which describes the care and feeding of a young plant so that it grows properly to maturity. In verses 7 and 8, Paul uses some distinctive words to describe what nurture really is in the eyeball-to-eyeball relationships that accompany leadership responsibility.

He speaks of being "gentle," the word *herioi,* used often of a teacher who is patient in the process of nurturing seemingly incorrigible students. As if that emphasis were not enough, he refers to the gentleness of a nurse, which is an obvious reference to a nursing mother, not a hired babysitter. The word is used in the Old Testament to describe Jehovah's care of Israel, and in 2 Timothy 2:24 Paul used the word to describe "the servant of the Lord."

But there is more to this emphasis on nurture. A gentle, nursing mother "cherisheth her children." The word is *thalpē,* which literally means "to soften by heat" or "to keep warm." Deuteronomy 22:6, in the Septuagint, uses the word to describe a bird caring for its young by spreading its feathers over them in the nest. Such a nurse is "affectionately desirous" of the growing children (v. 8), a term that seems cumbersome but appears in AV, ASV, and RSV texts. The implication is a yearning after for the good of the group, which ultimately results in, as this verse indicates, a sacrifice on the part of the leader.

Where is the manliness in all of this? Where is the image of the sharp voice barking orders and "running a tight ship"? Again, a pagan culture distorts our understanding of spiritual reality. We identify masculinity with toughness and ruggedness, but God identifies it with tenderness. We think of leadership as "handling" adults, but God thinks of it as nurturing children.

New Testament leadership is example

The hard work of Paul's leadership spills out in verse 9. Both day and night, with great effort, he worked among the believers. His own life and those of his colleagues were examples of holiness, justice, and blamelessness before God. Note that this was behavior *before the believers*, not an attempt at evangelism.

In chapter 2, verses 5 and 6, Paul assured the Thessalonians that their leaders were men, not some kind of superhuman, ecclesiastical giants who wanted to run the organization by sheer executive skill and personal power.

New Testament leadership is fatherhood

What does a father do? According to Ephesians 6:4, he is responsible for the nurture of children. Consequently, the model of the family is used not only to describe procreation in terms of infant birth, but also to describe leadership functions in terms of the teaching role of a father in the home.

In 1 Thessalonians 2:11, the words rendered *exhorted* and *comforted* are the words *parakalountes* and *paramuthoumenoi*. These are commonly used together in Paul's writing. The former is often used of divine ministry, but the latter is always a human word. It is never used directly to mean God's comfort but is descriptive of the way He uses people to minister to other people in the community of faith.

A father also "charges" his children (v. 11). The word has the idea of admonishing or witnessing truth so that they will walk in patterns acceptable to God.

Paul's Example

Earlier, we noted the positive pattern of Christ in leadership training. A word or two about the example of the apostle Paul may also be worth mentioning. The development of the New Testament church was the multiplication of the lives of the few people described in Acts 1. Many of the church leaders were personally trained by the apostle Paul. He was, in effect, the "pilot project." Timothy, Silas, Titus, Epaphroditus, the Ephesian elders, and many others were spin-offs from his own life and ministry.

There is, in some local churches today, the great curse of a one-man ministry, which looks much like the worldly leadership condemned by our Lord in Luke 22. If we are to serve our own generation with power and effectiveness, we must stop pretending that being a Christian leader is like being a king of the Gentiles.

2

The Gift of Administration

THE NEW TESTAMENT CHURCH has two dimensions to its existence. It is both an *organization* and *organism*. Because of its dual nature, the church faces two kinds of problems—*administrative* and *spiritual*. Too frequently, church leaders attempt to give spiritual answers to organizational problems and organizational answers to spiritual problems. The difficulty is compounded by some unfortunate misunderstandings of the nature of administration. Consider, for example, the following three myths:

1. Administration is nonessential. Some pastors think that the work of the local church will be carried on purely by an emphasis on pietistic endeavors, without a concern for the dreary, paper-shuffling tasks frequently associated with the work of administration.

2. Administration is uninteresting. After all, the real glory of Christian leadership is in preaching, teaching, counseling, and similar interpersonal ministries. Most people who hold this view would grudgingly agree that somebody has to handle the administration, but they have no inclination to offer an Isaiah-like "Here am I; send me" (Is 6:8).

3. Administration is not spiritual. Perhaps this is the most dangerous myth of all, for it attempts to drive a wedge between crucial ministries of the Christian leader. It suggests that some ministries are "sacred," and others are "secular."

Published as an article in *Church Administration*, 15:5, pp. 14-18. © Copyright 1972 The Sunday School Board of the Southern Baptist Convention. All rights reserved. Used by permission.

People who think this way tend to gravitate toward unbiblical views of church leadership because they misunderstand the crucial, New Testament function of administration as a spiritual gift.

ANALYSIS OF BIBLICAL BACKGROUNDS

The word used in the New Testament to describe the gift of administration is *kubernētēs*. It is the noun form of *kubernao*, which literally means, "to steer a ship." Although one passage in the New Testament is distinctive in helping us understand the gift, other passages in both the New Testament and the Septuagint (the Greek version of the Old Testament) provide significant, parallel information. Since the word appears only three times in the New Testament, it is not impossible to briefly examine each usage in this biblical analysis.

NEW TESTAMENT USES

Acts 27:11. The context of *kubernēsis* here is Paul's trip across the Mediterranean Sea to Rome. Although Paul predicts danger from the coming storm, the centurion pays no attention to the words of the prisoner but listens to the suggestion of the master of the ship. Here the emphasis is clearly on the idea of a helmsman. It was the responsibility of this ship administrator to know times of the day; the nature and direction of storms; the habits of air currents; the process of steering by the stars and sun; and, because of his knowledge, to correctly direct the ship.

Revelation 18:17. I have deliberately skipped over the passage which would appear second in chronological order, because the Revelation reference is so similar to the usage in Acts. Here, in a condemnatory poem spoken against historic and eschatological Babylon, John talks about the tremendous wealth of the city as viewed by tradesmen and "every shipmaster."

Perhaps one point about the above description should be

clarified. The helmsman is not to be thought of just as a man who obeyed orders and kept his hands on the wheel. He is, rather, the responsible decision-maker on the ship. He has complete charge of the vessel's activity, in behalf of the owner. As Kittel notes, "Sometimes he [the owner] engages only the *kubernētēs* and the *kubernētēs* the rest of the crew."[1] In effect, then, the *kubernētēs, or kubernēsis* (the words are virtually synonymous), is the captain of the ship.

1 Corinthians 12:28. It is this passage which clearly marks administration as a spiritual gift. Although the word *governments* is used in the text of the Authorized Version, our understanding of the process of administration is the most fitting concept of the word in present vocabulary. Kittel has a most helpful, descriptive paragraph, which relates *kubernēsis* to the other gifts which appear in the same passage.

> The reference can only be to the specific gifts which qualify a Christian to be a helmsman to his congregation, i.e., a true director of its order and therewith of its life. What was the scope of this directive activity in the time of Paul we do not know. This was a period of fluid development. The importance of the helmsman increases in a time of storm. The office of directing the congregation may well have developed especially in emergencies both within and without. The proclamation of the Word was not originally one of its tasks. The apostles, prophets and teachers saw to this. . . . No society can exist without some order and direction. It is the grace of God to give gifts which equip for government. The striking point is that when in v. 29 Paul asks whether all are apostles, whether all are prophets or whether all have gifts of healing, there are no corresponding questions in respect of *antilenpseis and kubernēsis.* There is a natural reason for this. If necessary, any member of the congregation may step in to serve as deacon or ruler. Hence these offices, as distinct from those mentioned in v. 29, may be elective. But this does not alter the fact that for their proper discharge the *charisma* of God is indispensable.[2]

OLD TESTAMENT USES (SEPTUAGINT)

Proverbs 1:5. Interestingly enough, most of the Old Testament uses of *kubernēsis* are in the book of Proverbs. The emphasis is closely related to the concept of wisdom, and denotes the ability of the leader to offer proper direction to his group. In this passage, Solomon suggests that the wise man will increase his knowledge, and one who has understanding will find proper direction to perceive the truth and act accordingly.

Proverbs 11:14. Where there is no proper administration, the people will fall. The dependence on clear-cut direction from a competent leader is a frequent theme in Solomon's writings.

Proverbs 24:6. This is a military context. Only with wise administration can one win a war, for, in the final analysis, wisdom rather than might prevails.

Ezekiel 27:8. This is similar to the Revelation passage, in that it speaks of the helmsman, the administrator of a ship.

SECULAR CONCEPTS OF ADMINISTRATION

In one of my books[3] I have dealt with the sociological context of administrative theory, and therefore shall not rework that material here. It is important, however, to offer a contrast between the biblical focus on administration as a gift of the Holy Spirit and the secular conceptions of management scientists.

There are at least three components in all administrative situations, and some leaders in the field recognize four. There is, of course, a *man* who brings to the administrative task his own personality and ability (or lack of it) as a decision maker, motivator, organizer, and leader of others. He will have a distinctive self-concept, which will greatly affect the work of administration which he handles. How the administrator sees himself as a leader will significantly determine his approach to almost every duty.

There is also the *work group*. This term is always a reference to the people with whom the administrator interacts on a regular basis. It may be a congregation; it may be a professional staff of subordinates; it may be a faculty; or it may even be students over whom one has a "helmsman" responsibility. It is toward the work group that the focus of this book will be directed, under the umbrella term *human relations*.

The third ingredient is generally described as the *situation* itself, but some writers derive a total of four components by dividing the situation into the *task* and the *organization. Task* is a reference to the organizational goals established by others, usually a board of directors. Occasionally the word *problem* is used to describe the task as the administrator sees it. The concept of *organization* may have two slants. At times it refers to the institution itself, describing constitution, bylaws, and lines of authority. It may also refer, in a more general sense, to the standard procedures of behavior and function within the institution, although these might not be prescribed in formal, written documents.

One of the best definitions of administration is also the simplest: *administration is getting things done through people.* Interaction among the three or four elements is a constant mixture of the carrying out of administrative tasks in any institution. We may be talking about a pastor, a Sunday school superintendent, a mission board executive, or a managerial consultant for General Motors. Since administration is a single science, each of these men faces similar tasks in attempting to achieve organizational goals by directing the activities of its people. Obviously, such a conclusion has some rather basic assumptions:

1. The organization has goals. These goals may not be written and may, indeed, not even be clearly understood by the constituency. Many Christians have distorted concepts of what the church is supposed to be and do in contemporary society. If the administrator is really a helmsman, the way he perceives of organizational goals dare not be fuzzy.

2. The organization has some structure to facilitate goal

achievement. It is this issue of structure which has become such a battleground for the church in the 1970s. How much structure is really prescribed for a Christian organization? Where are the fences between form and freedom? Here again, the administrator, whether pastor or bookstore manager, Sunday school superintendent or college dean, must thoroughly understand, if not initiate, structures and forms for the achievement of his organization's goals. At times these may be handed down to him from policy-making bodies, such as boards. At other times, those bodies will look to him to not only carry the water but first construct the pail.

3. The organization requires effective administration if goals are to be reached. Effective administration is not an option for the church any more than it is for AT & T. The administrator's position as a decision maker and group leader will either facilitate or hinder institutional goal-achievement.

Some writers in the area of management science attempt to make specific distinctions between the concepts of leadership and administration. James M. Lipham, for example, writing in *Behavioral Science and Educational Administration*, suggests that although leadership and administration have many factors in common, they are really mutually exclusive. Leadership, according to Lipham, has to do with changing organization goals. But administration is concerned with maintaining established structures.[4]

Such a narrow concept tends to further confuse already foggy notions about administration. All Lipham is doing is describing different administrative styles. It ought to be quite obvious that many administrators are very creative leaders, and the role of bringing about change is welcomed and competently handled. On the other hand, many administrators are "custodial managers" whose only concern is to "keep the lid on." In Lipham's own words, "Leadership functions and administrative functions are usually combined in a single role incumbent."[5]

The grouping of Lipham and other writers to pinpoint

the distinctives of administration is indicative of research
which emerged in the wake of the human relations movement
in management science. Following the Hawthorne studies,[6]
the emphasis in the second quarter of the twentieth century
was a rather extreme reaction to the failure of the "trait approach" to isolate significant leadership personality. Administration in those early years became almost exclusively the
ability to work with one's group.

In the sixties and seventies, however, contemporary research is recognizing that those who emphasized certain leadership traits as the basis for identification of administrative
roles may have had more of a point than the human relations
people allowed them to retain. Present emphasis, then, is one
of balance, recognizing the validity of individual traits (gifts
in the biblical sense), goal achievement and situational adap-
tation of leadership style.

DRAWING SOME PRACTICAL IMPLICATIONS

What help is there for harried administrators in an analysis
of the relationship between secular research and biblical
exegesis? Certainly, several themes emerge which properly
fit both the biblical and secular patterns:

1. The Christian leader's administrative style will depend
upon what he considers administration to be. If *kubernēsis*
is nothing more than paper shuffling, a necessary evil to the
continuing existence of the organization, then administration
will always appear unessential, uninteresting, and unspiritual.
If, on the other hand, the leader can view himself as a biblical captain of the ship handling its course and cargo in
stewardship for the heavenly owner, he certainly can approach his task with a dynamic and a spiritual enthusiasm
not often attached to the role of administration.

2. The blending of spiritual gifts and leadership roles has
evolved considerably since the days of the New Testament.
Kittel, in the lengthy paragraph quoted earlier, notes that
in the early church, administration was clearly essential. But

it was not usually the work of the apostles and prophets. Even by the time of Timothy and Titus, however, Paul was giving direction for activities which are basically administrative in function, such as widow rolls, leadership training responsibilities, and organization of congregational activities. It is probable that several men in any given congregation or organization will have the gift of administration. One of them may be the multigifted pastor who serves as main "helmsman." But if the pastor does not possess the gift of administration, he must seek out other men who do, and trust their judgment in matters of management.

3. The gift of administration is a capacity for learning executive skills, not a package of already developed skills. Of course, this is true of any spiritual gift. No sensible pastor would argue that he has no need to study, because he has the gift of teaching, and the Holy Spirit simply gives him things to say when he stands in the pulpit. Yet, while many pastors and other Christian leaders train extensively for preaching, teaching, and counseling ministries, most of them spend very little time in formal training (or even informal reading) to develop the capacity for administrative oversight. The gift of administration therefore suffers from "benign neglect."

4. The gift of administration is inseparably bound up with the process of working with people. Christian leaders must know how to get along with people. Developing and polishing human relations skills is a basic ingredient of successful administration. It will lead to understanding of the innate conflict between individual personality and institutional role. It will recognize the necessity for matching personnel utilization, in the church and other Christian organizations, with human interests and needs. Above all, it will emphasize a leadership style and concept of administration which focus on the community and *koinonia* of Christian groups not as a desirable approach, but as the crucial guideline by which biblical administration can be effectively judged.

3

Unity and Community in the Body

WHAT IS THE GREATEST PROBLEM the church faces today? Is it the threat to orthodox theology by a militant liberalism? Certainly that threat is always there, but evangelical churches seem to be much more troubled, in these declining years of the twentieth century, by the immature behavior of Christians *within* their ranks than they are by the heresy from *without*. The issues of ecclesiology are the battleground of the 1970s, and it is imperative that a book attempting to describe the biblical way that God's people work together in church ministries should emphasize the issues of unity and community within the body of Christ.

The theological concept of the universal church is a reference to the spiritual unity of all of the redeemed in all ages and places. It includes believers who are Jews or Gentiles, in heaven or on earth, and stretches historically from the origin of the church at Pentecost to the final day when we shall be in heaven with the Lord. The objective of that unity, as Paul clearly declares in Ephesians 1, is a common redemption through the atonement of Calvary and a collective demonstration of the grace and glory of Jesus Christ.

UNDERSTANDING THE CHURCH

The eternal and invisible unity of the universal church is made contemporary and visible in the form of local churches. It is precisely this concept which in recent years has created so much confusion and controversy with respect to definition

26

and description. Yet local churches have always been God's way of demonstrating the work of the universal church and, as one studies the New Testament, there seems to be at least a minimum boundary of inclusion which can be recognized by way of description of a local church. Writing out of the context of congregational polity, I would like to suggest that the local church is *a body of confessed believers joining together for worship, fellowship, instruction, and evangelism; led in their efforts by biblical officers (pastors and deacons); sovereign in polity; and including, as a part of its life and ministry, observance of the ordinances, discipline, and mutual edification.*

My colleague, Dr. Robert Culver, enumerates six characteristics of a local church: spiritual vitality, doctrinal instruction, fellowship, observance of the Lord's Supper, prayer, and Christian testimony.[1] The popular, contemporary apologist, Francis Schaeffer, indicates eight ingredients which must be a part of "the polity of the church as a church":

1. Local congregations made up of Christians
2. Special meetings on the first day of the week
3. Church officers (elders) who have responsibility for the local churches
4. Deacons responsible for the community of the church in the area of material things
5. A serious view of discipline
6. Specific qualifications for elders and deacons
7. A place for form on a wider basis than the local church
8. The observance of two sacraments, baptism and the Lord's Supper[2]

Many additional pages could be filled with a statement of various views as well as a biblical exposition of the nature of the universal church and the local church, but that is not the primary purpose of this volume. What is of concern is that the reader recognize the *validity and essentiality of the local church as a visible, contemporaneous demonstration of the universal church and the primary importance that unity and community be demonstrated in its interpersonal relations.*

A theological concept that is closely aligned here is the matter of the priesthood of believers. Actually, there are only five passages, in two books of the New Testament, which refer directly to the priesthood of believers—few enough that they can be reproduced here (from *The Living Bible*):

> And now you have become living building-stones for God's use in building his house. What's more, you are his holy priests; so come to him—[you who are acceptable to him because of Jesus Christ]—and offer to God those things that please him [1 Pe 2:5].

> But you are not like that, for you have been chosen by God himself—you are priests of the King, you are holy and pure, you are God's very own—all this so that you may show to others how God called you out of the darkness into his wonderful light [1 Pe 2:9].

> All praise to him who always loves us and who set us free from our sins by pouring out his life blood for us. He has gathered us into his kingdom and made us priests of God his Father. Give to him everlasting glory! He rules forever! Amen! [Rev 1:5b-6].

> "You are worthy to take the scroll and break its seals and open it; for you were slain, and your blood has bought people from every nation as gifts for God. And you have gathered them into a kingdom and made them priests of our God; they shall reign upon the earth" [Rev 5:9b-10].

> Blessed and holy are those who share in the First Resurrection. For them the Second Death holds no terrors, for they will be priests of God and of Christ, and shall reign with him a thousand years [Rev 20:6].

One writer draws from these Scriptures five principles which speak to the issue of the relationship of believers in community as they seek to worship and serve God together.

1. The priesthood of the believer must be held in healthy tension with other basic concepts; it is not an absolute.
2. The believer can delegate some of the authority of his life and ministry to other believers.
3. The priesthood of the believers is conditioned by the gifts and roles in the life of the fellowship.
4. The priesthood of the believer implies shared responsibility and ministry as well as shared authority.
5. The priesthood of the believer is the basis for decision making in the church.[3]

Such a commitment to shared responsibility and authority is based on a proper understanding of what it means to be the church, and leads, I would think, to the kind of participatory democracy described in the first two chapters of this book. It emphasizes again that we are indeed "laborers together," not only with God, but also with each other, in carrying out the tasks of the church and establishing its witness in the world in any given era of its history.

PAUL'S CONCEPT OF THE BODY

There is, perhaps, no visual idea of the church receiving more attention today than the image of the body described by Paul in the twelfth chapter of 1 Corinthians. On every hand, we hear about "body life" and "body truth" and the exercise of spiritual gifts within the body. This is surely a healthy emphasis. It will help us to look again at the primitive notions (primitive in the sense of being authentic) which the early church had of itself and at the cardinal principles which governed its life and ministry in the first century.

The first Corinthian epistle was probably written from Ephesus, about 57 A.D. Corinth was a metropolis of the Roman province of Achaia, and a great commercial center of the Mediterranean world. Paul had visited the city twice and found it living up to its reputation as a center of sin and depravity. Corinth presented an enormous challenge to the gospel. To expect the principles of Christian faith to operate at Jerusalem, where the members of the early church had been schooled for years in Old Testament truth, was one thing; to motivate that kind of behavior in pagan Corinth was quite another.

Deplorable factions had split the Corinthian church into hostile fragments. Some of the believers claimed to follow Paul, others Apollos, others Peter, and some claimed such a pharisaical piety that they wished to bypass all of the contemporary leaders and refer themselves directly back to Christ. Paul deals with a number of the problems resulting from the schism which was destroying the unity and community at Corinth, and in chapter twelve he comes to an explanation of the nature and use of spiritual gifts. Interestingly, however, the bulk of the chapter does not deal with the specification of the gifts but rather with the kind of people who will be ministering them. The words of the old hymn "Onward Christian Soldiers" well depict the intent of 1 Corinthians 12. They remind the church, "We are not divided; all one body we, One in hope and doctrine, One in charity."

Paul is well known for his use of common illustrations to explain difficult spiritual truths. First Corinthians 12 demonstrates in detail how the unity of man's *physical* body offers a model for the kind of unity that ought to be exemplified in Christ's *spiritual* body. In verse 13 the apostle points out that the purpose of the baptismal ministry of the Holy Spirit is to place persons into the universal body of Christ, the church. Most evangelical scholars agree that the treatment of *baptism* here is less likely a reference to the ritual act of water baptism than to the spiritual act of implantation into the body. It is always important to remember that symbolical acts exist only to emphasize spiritual reality.

What comes through, in the essence of this chapter, is the old philosophical principle, "The whole is greater than the sum of its parts." Diversity of the parts is an essential ingredient of the operating body, but unity and community of the members is what allows the body to function properly. Paul draws the argument to ridiculous extremes in order to make his point: "If the whole body were an eye, where were the hearing? If the whole were hearing, where were the smelling?" (v. 17). What kind of a functioning organism would one's body be if it were composed of nothing but one giant eye? Or perhaps one giant ear and no nose? Apparently, leaders exercising autocratic control were already manifesting their power in the early church. People whose strong personalities overwhelm the body of Christ and dominate its life and ministry have plagued the church from the first century until now. Such overpowering control by one member shows an inaccurate concept of what the church is.

After he focuses our attention on the functions of the physical body, Paul nails down the argument which is really his intent in this section of the epistle: *God has a place for everyone in the church, and everyone's place is important.* Remember the context of the passage, the issue of spiritual gifts. Every Christian has a spiritual gift, and some may have more than one. And just as all of the members have spiritual gifts, all of the members have distinct functions. God has gifted people for carrying on the work of the church and then placed them in the body for a particular purpose of ministry. Not only that, but He has done it in His own divine sovereignty, just as He arranged the organs of the physical body to create the best possible working relationship! Only when all of the members of the physical body are doing their task does that body function properly. The same is true of the church.

Distortion of the concepts of unity and community comes when some fail to exercise their proper gifts and roles in the body, or when certain members of the body are considered to be weaker or stronger, more necessary or less necessary, than others. When there is mutual care in the body, discord can be eliminated, but a ruptured organ can destroy the proper functioning of the system. An oversized gland creates ab-

normality, and the entire organism (or organization) suffers
desperately.

In verse 26, Paul points out that there is perhaps no time
in which the unity of the body is more apparent than during
a time of pain or suffering. A broken leg sends splinters of
pain throughout the entire system. Even the common cold
can produce, at the same time, a runny nose, red and tired
eyes, an earache, an aching head, a sore throat, an upset
stomach, and general discomfort throughout the entire body.

In the same way, all of the members of the body of Christ
share the suffering and unhappiness of any one of the members. Since the body is a unity which shares community,
when one of its members is feeling well or enjoying some
particular benefits, the entire body rejoices. This is true
physically of the human body and spiritually of the church.
In another place Paul wrote, "Rejoice with them that do rejoice, and weep with them that weep" (Ro 12:15).

The crucial application comes in verse 27 of our chapter:
"Now ye are the body of Christ, and members in particular."
Note the emphasis on the word *ye*. Even this fractured Corinthian church, with all of its doctrinal confusion and personal bickering, was a demonstration in the world of the body
of Christ! The "bookends" of this passage fit the classic
Pauline logic: "For as the body is one" (v. 12) and, "Now ye
are the body" (v. 27). Alan Redpath suggests that the kind
of unity which Paul insists on in this chapter "is only possible as we recognize that within the church we have fellowship in our diversity, as we learn to love and to care for our
brethren who are different, always recognizing the utter
futility of identity."[4]

Francis Schaeffer speaks often about community. He emphasizes that horizontal relationship can only follow vertical
relationship, because a Christian community can only be
made up of individual Christians.

Therefore, as we meet in our groups, we know who we are. We are not like those who march in our streets and do not know who they are—who call for community but have no basis for community beyond biological continuity. Now we are ready to begin real personal living, to practice the orthodoxy of community corporately as a community. Real personal Christian living individually and corporately as a community that rests upon the individual's and the community's personal relationship with a personal God gives us the possibility of Christian community before the eye of an observing world.[5]

THE IMPLEMENTATION OF UNITY AND COMMUNITY

It would be delightful to spend the rest of the chapter continuing the discussion of the biblical nature of the "comm-united" church. But this is a book about human relations and personnel practice. Up to this point, I have tried to lay a biblical foundation for the drawing of some implications as to the kind of human relationships we must maintain if we are to work together harmoniously and effectively in the church or in other Christian organizations. Now let me deal briefly with four concepts which help to form a pattern of ministry which is based, if not on specific verses of 1 Corinthians 12, at least upon the general New Testament concept of the church as a unified body. There are, of course, a multitude of other Scriptures which could be brought to bear upon the issues.

A PEOPLE-CENTERED MINISTRY

In one sense it is correct to say that the church is the most person-centered organization in the world (or at least should be). In quite another sense, the church must be God-centered before it can be person-centered. Finding the proper balance between these two very important ingredients of biblical life has proven too great a responsibility for some churches, and they have slipped from the path either to the left (an overemphasis on humanism to the neglect of the sovereignty of God) or to the right (a position which uses a "burden for souls" as an excuse for a lack of consideration of people's needs).

The biblical pattern of Christian love always finds its out-working within the context of relationships with people. Yet it is precisely at this point that so many Christian leaders and workers go sour. Many of our problems testify not so much to our inability to perform effectively in public minis-tries, as to our inability to get along with people in private, interpersonal relations. The church is and always has been *people*, and service in it at any given time is a necessary rela-tionship with those people. Adequate leadership requires awareness of and sensitivity to human need all around us as well as an appreciation of how we can meet that need through the supernatural dynamics of God's truth and God's Spirit.

Consider, for example, a pastor who finds his own self-satis-faction and fulfillment amidst the books in his study, where he spends all of his time. Although his theology may be or-thodox and his sermons scholarly, the dimension of reality could be missing from his ministry. His lifeline to meaning-ful ministry is in constant contact with *people*, so that he can learn to relate God's truth to real problems in real lives.

Our Lord's ministry was always centered on people, and, without doubt, He was primarily interested in meeting their spiritual and eternal needs. But this priority focus did not keep Him from showing an interest in temporal and physical needs as well. If the various bodily parts are going to func-tion properly together, it will be because we have been able to discover and implement a new-covenant view of interper-sonal relations.

THE GIFT OF LEADING

In conjunction with the gift of administration (*kubernē-sis*), there is also a concept of leadership which appears in

Romans 12:8, which uses the word *prohistēmi.** It literally
means "put before" or "to go before." Originally it had the
connotation of presiding, conducting, directing, or governing.
I have often asked myself whether *kubernēsis* and *prohistēmi*
represent two different spiritual gifts or two dimensions of
the same spiritual gift, namely, congregational leadership.
As closely as these ideas are linked, it may be preferable to
think of leadership as merely one of the functions of the administrator.

In spite of the leadership role's accompanying prestige and
necessary publicity, the New Testament concept of leadership is service. Those who exercise the gift of leadership
and administration—the professional church staff and those
who occupy significant, nonprofessional offices—are examples
to the body. Somehow, a balance between delegated authority and loving concern must be the primary goal for biblical
administration.

D. Swan Haworth identifies three interesting concepts of
staff relationships:

1. A loosely organized staff which may have several "solo-
   ists" but no director, no regular rehearsals, and consequently very little harmony; people on such a staff relate
   to each other only by necessity
2. An integrated staff held together by one commander
3. A colleague relationship in which "each staff member
   trusts the other, despite their differences. This colleague
   relationship requires each member of the team to be a
   responsible person."⁶

It is quite obvious that the relationships of the professional
staff stand as a model for the entire church. Confusion and
bickering at the top will not only destroy the working effectiveness of the management team, but will filter down into
the ranks to distort interpersonal relationships between other
workers all the way up and down the line.

*For other appearances of *prohistēmi* see 1 Th 5:12; 1 Ti 3:4, 12; 5:17;
Titus 3:8, 14.

THE REQUIREMENT OF A BIBLICAL LIFE-STYLE

The Christian leader's behavior toward other people is determined by what he is in himself. To put it another way, interpersonal relations on a horizontal plane are determined by interpersonal relations with God on a vertical plane. One of the reasons we get into so many human relations problems in the church is that we have somehow confused ourselves into thinking that what we *do* for God is more important than what we *are* before God. A distinctly Christian life-style, with respect to shared ministries in a communal setting, requires the grace of mutual acceptance, a willingness to enter into mutual burden-bearing, and a generous dose of active love.

Understanding one's fellow workers involves seeing and knowing them as persons rather than as "other employees." Paul Tournier points out two great fears which keep people from understanding each other: fear of being judged and fear of being advised.[7] Harsh criticism and flippant answers to troubling problems are two clubs which can bludgeon human relations to a bloody hulk. For example, some adults have no ministry with teenagers because they greet every attempt at communication with a handy, "Oh yes, I used to feel like that. You'll get over it."

The immorality of manipulation is not confined to Madison Avenue. If manipulation is an immoral technique, it is just as wrong for the church leader as it is for the advertising executive whose task it is to design television commercials geared to trick people into buying what they do not need.

In our pressure-cooker society, it is extremely difficult to grasp and practice the biblical concept of patience. We tend to be obsessive and compulsive about our behavior, and frequently "come on too strong" in relationships with other people. I like the way one writer puts it: "Impatience is a heresy of the soul and an apostasy of the disposition."[8]

Schaeffer calls unity in love "the mark of the Christian"

(in the book by that title) and refers to that unity as "the final apologetic." He points out that the world cares nothing for doctrine, but has been given the authority to judge the effectiveness and authenticity of the church on the evidence of a loving life-style among the members in its community.

UNDERSTANDING INTERPERSONAL ENCOUNTER

In one sense, we can think of the whole social order as a communications framework. If unity and community are to be realized, the third concept of communication (a term obviously related to the first two) must be functioning properly. Communication can be verbal or nonverbal, and should not be confused with the information theory of hardware and software systems. Some sociologists (the symbolic interactionists) remind us that no one person can be held responsible for communication; it is always a mutual process. The word *mutuality* becomes very important in recognizing the interrelated nature of communication.

CONTEXT OF SENDING
AND RECEIVING
CONTEXT OF SENDING
AND RECEIVING

IDEAS

WORDS

WORDS ARE THE VEHICLES BY WHICH IDEAS
ARE TRANSPORTED.

Another term frequently used in sociological literature is *simultaneity*. Communication is not like a Ping-Pong game, in which messages are batted back and forth. Rather, the ongoing relationship between people who are communicating is a simultaneous process. If we would effectively relate to other people, we must recognize that our verbalizations to them and their verbalizations to us are all received through an emotional and cultural grid.

When a Sunday school superintendent, for example, speaks to one of his teachers, the meaning of his words is not so much inherent in what he says, as it is in the way that she interprets them by placing her own meanings upon them. These two people are simultaneously active in the communications process and are therefore mutually responsible for what happens in their personal interaction. Each is loading up little trucks (words) with cargo (ideas) and sending them on their way. At the same time, each is unloading the trucks sent to him by the other person.

The main assumption of sociology is that human beings develop their human abilities through social interaction, and the community of church, school, or other institution provides the context for an analysis of relationships. We might also add that it provides the context for positive functioning together of believers as the body of Christ, in keeping with the kind of patterns delineated in 1 Corinthians 12 and other passages of the New Testament. We are certainly not passive recipients of everything that sociology and psychology tell us about human relationships. But we must be astute discerners of truth and willing to apply it as it fits our understanding of the special revelation of the Word of God.

Perhaps this chapter should end where it began, with some treatment of the church. Surely, any recognition of styles of relationship must stand under a proper delineation of the Lordship of Christ. Walter Liefeld has written:

> A local church . . . functions as a body of disciples devoted

to their Lord and transmitting His teaching. The church remembers the past, insofar as it reminds itself and the world of its origin in the death and resurrection of Christ. It faces the future as an eschatological community in which the characteristics of the kingdom and the presence of the king are realized in its daily life.[9]

4

Personnel Selection and Supervision

THERE IS, in Christian ministry, a dynamic tension that must be maintained between the concepts of *gift* and *call*. We know from the New Testament that the Holy Spirit sovereignly gives to every Christian a spiritual gift which He intends for that individual to use in the service of Christ through the church. Some Christian leaders are given multiple gifts, and there seems to be evidence that these are the persons then called into positions of professional leadership in the various ministries of the church, both in its local congregations and in its outreach in education, literature, and world mission. An individual properly understands his relationship to the whole concept of Christian service only when he understands his spiritual gift and develops its capacity for implementation.

But the other dimension, the concept of call, is rather like the rudder that steers the ship. None of the spiritual gifts delineated in the New Testament has any geographical connotation. No one, for example, has the gift of "missionary work in Africa" or "ministry to inner city youth." The gift, rather, describes the what of ministry, and the call then designates the where of ministry. That is why we should not be upset when a missionary who has been ministering, let us say, in Germany, may decide at one point that it is within the will of God for him to switch to a ministry among German-speaking people in Argentina.

It is quite obvious that those who have the responsibility

of supervision and administration of people in collective ministry must recognize both of these crucial ingredients as biblical components. Sunday school superintendents must consider the necessity of the gift of teaching in their staff members, and also impress upon them the issue of being called to that specific kind of local-church ministry rather than to club work, music ministry, or youth leadership. Both Peter and Paul had multiple gifts for Christian ministry, certainly including the gift of proclamation (prophecy). But Paul was distinctly called to utilize his gift as an itinerant missionary-evangelist establishing new churches among the Gentiles, whereas Peter was given the responsibility of leading congregations of Jewish Christians.

The concepts of *gift* and *call*, if taken seriously, have profound implications for the way we recruit workers in the church or Christian organization, the way we supervise their activities, and the way we evaluate their performance. It is the intent of this chapter to explore some of those implications.

Developing a Christian Concept of Work and Ministry

One of the most interesting books I have ever encountered on the subject of leadership and administration is Abraham Zaleznik's *Human Dilemmas of Leadership.* Zaleznik's concern is the relation of an individual to his organization, and he writes out of a purely secular, industrial-management context.

Perhaps the key concept of the book has to do with the author's acceptance of human tension and conflict as a condition of existence and an opportunity for change and progress in the interrelationships between the individual and his organization. His psychoanalytical framework, with emphasis on Freud and Piaget, drifts far from a biblical frame of reference. Nevertheless, he explores some of the crucial issues, such as conflicts in work, authority and self-esteem, subordination, equality, rivalry, status, group formations, and other problems common to the relationship between an individual and the institution in which he serves.

What we have often failed to recognize in the church is that these problems do not exist only in the management-labor relations of the UAW or Teamsters. These same issues are among the cardinal points of difficulty in interpersonal relations in a Christian publishing house, an evangelical college or seminary, and a local church.

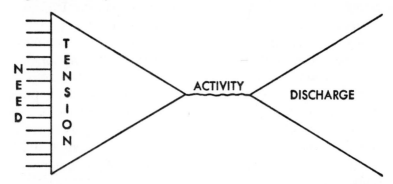

Interestingly enough, Zaleznik attacks what he calls "the Utopian View" of man's nature, denying that man is inherently good and rejecting the idea that the natural course of human life is toward personal growth or self-actualization. He substitutes his own position, which he dubs "the Individualistic View," emphasizing man's capability and the necessity for assuming responsibility in the work relationships. According to Zaleznik, the historic model of work is threefold: tension represents a need, activity results from the tension, and a discharge results from the gratifications of the action. Both rivalry and equality are developmental crises for the individual.

It is impossible for an organization to solve this problem, but it can "foster the ideals that make the developmental gains worth pursuing." Perhaps the most significant sentence in the book is the author's perceptive analysis of the key problem in personnel relations:

The unsolved problem in understanding man in organization centers around the inability of existing theory to grasp the essential dynamics of the individual, and from this understanding to formulate a true psychosocial theory of organization and leadership.[1]

Now what does all of this have to do with a Christian view of work and ministry? Simply this. Zaleznik has identified the crucial problem as *a misunderstanding on the part of all existing, secular theories in analyzing the nature of man, his understanding of himself, and his relationship to other people.* Unfortunately, Zaleznik, with his neutral view of human nature, also misunderstands the issue, and, as in all rejections of revelational truth, ends up with a perverted concept of reality. The fact of the matter is that man is neither good nor neutral, but essentially evil in his moral nature, as an abundance of biblical evidence clearly demonstrates.

The Christian view of man, so often characterized as being a *low* view, is, rather, in its totality a very *high* view of man. The Bible teaches that man was created in the image of God, and Christians are bona fide members of His family. Even the Christian administrator who is involved with personnel supervision in a secular organization must understand that the persons under his leadership are *potential* restored images and are therefore deserving of a genuinely Christian treatment (Col 4:1).

There is another important factor in a Christian view of work and ministry. In Christian service there are no menial jobs. Many contemporary psychologists have shown us (even though their views are most frequently not based on a biblical philosophy) that the foundation for a sense of well-being and meaning in life is not so much a matter of external circumstances, as it is a person's deep-down belief that he is indeed a worthy human being. In other words, rather than the menial job thrusting its impersonal clutches of despair upon the individual, the person recognizes the dynamics of gift and call and responds in a totally renewed way to what-

ever job he might have (Col 3:22-25). Call it a Christian
work-ethic if you will, but do not identify it with Puritanical
capitalism, for in contemporary society that is the kiss of
death.

But there is more at stake than just the worker's attitude
toward himself. That attitude is influenced by the administrative style of his supervisor. The Survey Research Center
at the University of Michigan conducted a national survey of
more than 1500 workers. This survey was analyzed in the
January 1972 issue of *Manpower*, a publication of the U.S.
Department of Labor. Some of the findings are most interesting. For example, construction workers and the self-employed
were at the top of the contentment scale, with only about one
in twenty registering dissatisfaction with his job. In technical, professional, and managerial occupations, the dissatisfaction rate was about ten percent but it climbed to twenty-five
percent for workers in service occupations and in the whole-
sale-retail industry. Among workers with low incomes, college experience was a real handicap to attaining job satisfaction.

Generally in the survey, women were shown to be more
dissatisfied with their jobs than men, and age did not seem
to be a significant factor in that dissatisfaction. Marriage,
however, was a strategic component, since unmarried young
people were twice as likely to be dissatisfied with their lives
as their married counterparts.

Perhaps the most significant finding, for those of us concerned with church ministries, was the seeming lack of emphasis on the matter of salary. Of the five work features rated
"most important," only one had to do with tangible or economic benefits. Indeed, ranked higher than salary levels were
"interesting work," "enough help and equipment to get the
job done," and "enough authority to get the job done."
Church leaders who constantly work with volunteer personnel should pay attention to the inherent message of those
statistics.

To hark back for just a moment to the previous chapter, the emphasis of the twelfth chapter of 1 Corinthians reinforces the concept that there are no menial jobs in Christian service. Given the human value-system and the cultural priorities of our society, certain ministries, like certain jobs, appear to be more important and prestigious. But in God's value system, all parts of the body are equally important, and all must be functioning at acceptable levels if unity and collective health are to be maintained.

In the helpful volume, *Counseling in an Organization,* Roethlisberger and Dickson identify what they call "five basic concerns" of employees:[2]

1. Keeping a job
2. Friendship and belonging
3. Felt injustices
4. Authority
5. Job and individual development

These concerns, the authors tell us, stem from three sources: company requirements, group values and norms, and individual needs. If we can "Christianize" the Roethlisberger and Dickson research by recognizing spiritual needs and sin as a part of that third concern, we may have a workable model by which to analyze our understanding of a Christian view of work and ministry. Such a model can help us identify the kind of managerial attitudes and administrative styles church leaders bring to their important tasks.

Securing and Serving Volunteer Workers

Notice the double emphasis in the heading above. We know that the responsible Christian administrator has the task of recruiting workers. But as I have tried to show in chapter one, a New Testament style of leadership requires that he see himself as their *servant* rather than their *lord* once they have become members of the ministry team. Surely the difference between paid employees and volunteer workers is an irrelevant factor here. It seems to me that there is a distinctive kind of managerial technique which one employs if he is committed to both successful functioning of the organization and biblical norms.

• Perhaps the following four guidelines represent a mixture of competent administrative science and Christian philosophy of leadership.

EVALUATE YOUR RECRUITMENT PROCESS

How are you now going about the matter of securing workers? Is your leadership largely dependent upon what Andrew Halpin calls "initiating structure"? Or do you emphasize the other end of the continuum, consideration? According to research in administration, the most effective leaders are those who score high in *both* dimensions of leadership behavior.

We must avoid being so intent upon getting a job done that we forget we are dealing with human beings, not cogs in the machine. At the same time, we want to steer away from the leadership style which may ooze with the milk of human kindness but contributes little to effective performance because there is no commitment to the initiation of structure and the pursuit of objectives in the organization.

In a real sense, a local-church board of Christian education functions as a personnel department in the recruitment and maintenance of workers. Board members are fallible and therefore must evaluate their recruitment activities in conjunction with certain basic questions: Are we recognizing gifts and calls? Are we emphasizing the meeting of individual needs? Are we avoiding the creation of concerns that trouble workers?

EMPHASIZE STRENGTHS IN JOB PLACEMENT

If Peter Drucker's book, *The Effective Executive*, is not the best book on management, it is certainly among the best. And one of the most significant chapters in that volume is the one entitled "Making Strength Productive." The initial paragraph warrants reproduction here:

The effective executive makes strengths productive. He knows that one cannot build on weakness. To achieve results one has to use all the available strengths—the strengths of associates, the strengths of the superior, and one's own strengths. These strengths are the true opportunities. To make strength productive is the unique purpose of organization. It cannot, of course, overcome the weaknesses with which each of us is abundantly endowed. But it can make them irrelevant. Its task is to use the strength of each man as a building block for joint performance.[3]

One of the rubrics Drucker offers in the chapter is the suggestion, "Effective executives know that they have to start with what a man can do rather than with what a job requires."[4] That implies getting the right man for the right job in staffing any organization, including a Sunday school or youth society in the local church.

In terms of the worker's response, we are faced again with the important factor of a positive self-concept based upon a biblical understanding of one's gift and call. The creative Christian in a world of challenge can never be content with the desires of Sancho Panza, in *Don Quixote*, who wished to be lord of an island if it were offered to him "with little trouble and less danger." Nor, of course, does he wish to follow the frenetic neuroticism of Sancho's lord and spend his days of service tilting at windmills. Somewhere between lies that happy, median ground of sane and scriptural ministry as the utilization of divine power through a human instrument.

APPRAISE POTENTIAL LEADERSHIP

Good leadership always breeds leadership—that is the thrust of what we have come to call the "Paul-Timothy approach." The effective Christian administrator has the task of assessing and recording how well each worker performs in his present position, and what kind of ability he demonstrates for other tasks. To be specific, which of the teachers in the primary department has the potential of becoming a depart-

mental superintendent? Which of the departmental superintendents would make a competent general superintendent?
Who are the potential deacons who will give leadership to
the congregation?

Effective appraisal of potential leadership is only possible when three basic, managerial functions are properly
operating:

1. Individual workers have a clear-cut knowledge of their
   roles in the organization.
2. Objectives and goals (including reasonable time lines)
   are established for measuring orderly results.
3. Regular, personal interaction is available for the discussion of mutual problems and progress.

DEVELOP ADEQUATE PERSONNEL POLICIES

The term *personnel policies* is simply a handy label to
describe the guidelines affecting the dealings which supervisors have with subordinates in an organization. Positive
personnel policies (if the presuppositions of this book are
valid) center on a biblical view of man, a biblical understanding of the importance of the individual in the institutional framework, and a biblical commitment to the strategic
position of the "gift-call" analysis of ministry. Such policies
should be clearly defined and understood by the workers, so
that they will not suffer from that organizational disease
sometimes called normlessness—an expectancy that socially
unapproved behaviors are required to achieve given goals.

In the volunteer organization, we are not dealing primarily
with pay raises, promotions, and attractive retirement benefits. We are, however, dealing with the problems of isolation,
self-estrangement, and the inability of an individual to
achieve his own goals while helping his organization to
achieve *its* goals. Positive personnel supervisors will emphasize development of meaningful relations, competent administration, encouragement of employee participation at all

points in the decision-making process, and a high level __ flexibility in the organization's roles and expectations.

FUNCTIONING IN THE ROLE OF SUPERVISOR

In an earlier work, I have defined supervision as "the directing of the activities of other people toward the accomplishment of organizational goals."[5] In that same chapter, it is suggested, that "a democratic view of leadership will emphasize the sharing of responsibility and the team-work aspect of serving together for Christ." It is also suggested that adequate supervision in any kind of educational situation includes at least six elements: placement, observation, evaluation, feedback, resource, and involvement.

It is my intention here to build on the concepts developed in my previous book, rather than just reiterating them in a different way. Perhaps that building can best be done by pointing out several principles of management which must be followed if a supervisor is going to adequately handle his task.

THE SUPERVISOR MUST PRACTICE ADEQUATE ADMINISTRATIVE PROCESS

There are certain, universally recognized essentials to efficient management and administration. These are applicable not only to the executives at General Motors but also to Sunday school superintendents, directors of Christian education, or pastors:

1. A clear and well-understood chain of command
2. Clearly defined lines of authority and responsibility
3. Elimination of overlapping authority, overstaffing, and duplication of function
4. Delegation of responsibility, including sufficient authority to carry out that responsibility
5. Simplification of executive function and procedure

6. Ability to make the optimum decision in the shortest possible time

7. The ability not only to get things done, but to do the right things

The implementation of these guidelines in the church should not lead us to the hard-nosed kind of executive power that is exhibited among "the kings of the Gentiles." When practiced in love, they may very well produce a blend of spiritual fervor and administrative competence that is precisely what we need in order to be the church in the contemporary world.

The supervisor must facilitate goal achievement

Some popular Christian leaders have disavowed the idea of objectives and goals. But a careful analysis of what they have said will generally lead to the conclusion that they are reacting largely against a church "numerology" in which God's people are constantly taken up with determining how many bodies they can pack into a given building in a given amount of time. A proper concept of goal setting and "management by objectives" is much more broad, and focuses upon personal, spiritual, and educational goals without forgetting the importance of the numerical dimension.

Robert D. Smith, associate professor of management at Kent State University, has written an excellent article applying these concepts to church organizations.
He argues:

> Managers who adopt a Management by Objectives (MBO) strategy feel that human beings perform more effectively if they know what is expected of them; that the overall effectiveness of the system will increase if all participants are aware of and committed to the desired results; that commitment can best be obtained through participation; and that expected performance should be defined and understood by all participants in the system.[6]

He discusses the dramatic changes now occurring in management science, and warns us:

> Leaders of the religious community will not be exempted from these changes. Church leaders of coming decades must be able to clearly identify the goals of their organization and subsequently set tangible, achievable, and challenging goals for themselves. They must likewise be able to help subordinates set compatible goals.[7]

THE SUPERVISOR MUST MAINTAIN QUALITY IN WORKER PERFORMANCE

How do you as supervisor evaluate and rate your workers? By their personality? By their past performance? By the amount of work which they can accomplish in a given amount of time? By their faithfulness? By their loyalty to the institution?

Most professional, employee-measuring programs depend upon an annual interview, the filling out of forms, and a general, subjective judgment on the part of supervisors. Although it is supposed to help the employee develop his skill and ability, the system usually does not work, because it is too often focused on the trait approach of leadership. The problem of adequate measurement of traits becomes almost insuperable.

Furthermore, most supervisors dislike the appraisal interview system, are hesitant to observe employees while they are performing their jobs, and do not like to sign their names to permanent records which might offer negative information about a subordinate. Frequently the forms are filled out and then forgotten.

What, then, is a satisfactory system of analyzing and enhancing worker performance?

Perhaps the best answer is not to forget these traditional factors of performance appraisal, but rather to improve the timing factor, which is what complicates the process. In other words, rather than an annual report, in which we try to

reach back to analyze what a teacher or editor was doing ten
or eleven months ago, constant communication between supervisor and subordinate should be the standard procedure
in any administrative system. Immediate praise is a reinforc-
ing factor, and prompt correction may keep the worker from
habituating an erroneous practice. Discuss achievement when
achievement occurs, and shortcomings when shortcomings
occur.

THE SUPERVISOR MUST LEARN HOW TO HANDLE GRIEVANCES

In today's revolutionary society, it is not difficult to imagine
workers at the local factory marching on strike, and carrying
placards which read:

> We demand meaningful work.
> We want to be plugged in.
> We demand responsibility.

Such a situation is not likely to occur among Sunday school
teachers in an evangelical church, but they may very well
be *thinking* things which they would never write on signs.
What *is* happening is that teachers and workers tend to just
give up when they become disenchanted with the institution or their work in it.

A supervisor's response to worker grievances may very
well retain the employee or alienate him completely. He must
understand precisely what the worker's complaint is, if there
is a satisfactory basis for the complaint, and if there is any
precedent, in the organization, for handling this kind of complaint. It is important to assure the worker that prompt attention will be given to the issue and that corrections will be
made if the organization is wrong.

Frequently it may be a matter of misunderstanding which
can be cleared up by a careful explanation of institutional
policy. On other occasions, it may be a clear-cut policy disagreement which must be understood in the light of the
worker's emotional and social context. In the Christian or-

ganization, a grievance may very well stem from spiritual immaturity or sin in the life of the worker or the supervisor. The sources of grievances may be organizational or spiritual, and we should not make the mistake of giving organizational answers to spiritual problems and spiritual answers to organizational problems.

THE SUPERVISOR MUST CUT DOWN ON RESIGNATIONS

This is obviously the next level of responsibility in the matter of dealing with grievances. *I quit* are words heard too frequently in Christian service, and particularly in the local church. Yet the words of Jeremiah the prophet haunt us in our contemporary situation: "His word was in my bones like a roaring fire, I was tired of trying to hold back, and I simply could not quit" (Jer 20:9, author's paraphrase).

We are told that in the secular employee-market, the rate at which employees resign or are dismissed from jobs in some companies and locations is more than 100% a year. Perhaps an even more pressing problem is the people who do not leave the organization but continue at their jobs disgruntled, unhappy, and making themselves and everyone about them constantly miserable.

This entire book is an attempt to answer the problem of resignations. To be specific, the key to retaining good workers may be summed up in three words: *challenge, recognition,* and *reward.* We must recognize that the worker needs opportunity to pursue *individual* goal achievement as well as to assist in *institutional* goal achievement. He needs participation in decision making, and a recognition that he is an important part of the organization. To put it another way, he must understand that his gifts and call are very much a part of the functioning body, and that the role which he is fulfilling is a strategic one.

All of the information provided from administrative science needs to be filtered through a theological sieve if it is to be applicable in the life and ministry of the Christian administrator. Perhaps the key concept of a genuinely biblical work ethic, to be followed by supervisors and subordinates alike, is found in the words of the apostle Paul in Ephesians 6:6-7: "Don't work hard only when your master is watching and then shirk when he isn't looking; work hard and with gladness all the time, as though working for Christ, doing the will of God with all your hearts" (TLB).

5

Bureaucracy and the Christian Organization

ONE OF THE OUTSTANDING THINKERS and writers in the area of management science is Dr. Chris Argyris, a management psychologist whose writings center on the relationship of the individual to his organization. Argyris argues that an individual's internal drive toward achievement, independence, and self-determination is basically characteristic of human nature, and therefore the goals of the administrator (and other workers, such as teachers) will be achieved if enough freedom is given for the development of that drive. This concept is in line with McGregor's Theory Y, which claims that people genuinely *do* want to achieve, and do not need to be forced into patterns of work, if those patterns are meaningful.

According to Argyris, society today expects early maturity and independence, which foster demand for participation in decision making. The term he uses for this increased power to the worker is "job enlargement." He points out that either the leadership style of the administrator and the self-concept of the worker may cause a major clash in the organization, or they can be brought together in creative tension to offer significant productivity. In his research on the problem, Argyris developed his findings in the terms of three propositions:

1. There is a lack of congruency between the needs of healthy individuals and the demands of the formal organization.

55

2. The results of this disturbance are frustration, failure, short time perspective, and conflict.
3. The nature of the formal principles of organization cause the subordinate, at any given level, to experience competition, rivalry, and intersubordinate hostility, and to develop a focus toward the parts rather than the whole.

The basic problem is a suffocating of independence and creativity which can be solved only by what Argyris calls a

> reduction in the degree of dependency, subordination, submissiveness, and so on experienced by the employee in his work situation. It can be shown that job enlargement and employee-centered (or democratic, or participative) leadership are elements which, if used correctly, can go a long way toward ameliorating the situation.[1]

In these days of reaction against "the system," the church has become a part of the firing line. Unfortunately, its place on that line is frequently that of target rather than gun-control officer. At the 1972 NAE convention in St. Louis, David Wilkerson chided the established church for a lack of flexibility in its program and said, "The established churches are more interested in their own little programs than in miracles; it has always been that way. If it isn't in the constitution and bylaws of the church, it is not recognized or accepted." In expressing such an attitude, Wilkerson only verbalized what many evangelicals in the youth subculture have been saying to their college and seminary professors for several years.

Is the church really a part of the bureaucracy? As a matter of fact, what is bureaucracy? Is it always bad? Is it possible for the church to disassociate itself from this "bureaucratic establishmentarianism"? These are some of the issues we want to explore in this chapter.

CHARACTERISTICS OF BUREAUCRACY

Most management scientists agree on some basic charac-

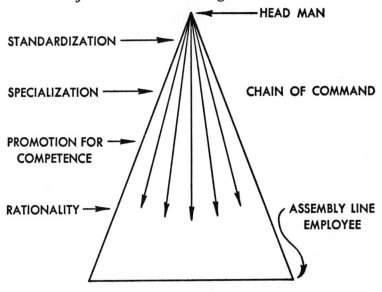

STANDARDIZATION

SPECIALIZATION

PROMOTION FOR
COMPETENCE

RATIONALITY

HEAD MAN

CHAIN OF COMMAND

ASSEMBLY LINE
EMPLOYEE

CHARACTERISTICS OF BUREAUCRACY

teristics of bureaucratic organizations. They do not always use the same words to describe these characteristics, nor are the lists always alike. Bureaucracy is basically a pyramid-shaped chain of command. Its interlocking facets create the red tape and waste that we so often associate with large organizations. What happens is that personalization and responsibility get lost in the complexity of the organization.

The following five ingredients of bureaucracy are eclectically derived from the writings of Bennis, Argyris, Blau, Weber, and others who have studied this phenomenon on the American scene.

STANDARDIZATION

The routine of work in a bureaucracy emphasizes the similarity of everybody's problems. Continuity of procedure is record-centered, and there exists a system of procedures and rules for dealing with all contingencies relating to work activities. The regular activities required to achieve the purposes of the organization have been distributed in a fixed way as "official duties."

SPECIALIZATION

Bureaucracy is basically task-centered so that it can deal with the kinds of skill developed through practice. The framers of the Industrial Revolution emphasized the concentration of effort upon a limited field of endeavor with a view toward increasing both the quality and quantity of output. It should follow, therefore, that organizational and administrative efficiency can also be increased by the specialization of tasks assigned to the participants of the organization. In the chapter indicated above, Argyris identifies three assumptions inherent in this underlying presupposition:

> The first is that the human personality will behave more efficiently as the task that it is to perform becomes specialized. Second is the assumption that there can be found a one best way to define the job so that it is performed at greater speed. Third is the assumption that any individual differences in the human personality may be ignored by transferring more skill and thought to machines.[2]

AUTHORITY IN THE HIERARCHY

Blau prefers the above term, while both Bennis and Argyris speak of a "chain of command." Basically, this is visualized in the form of the old pyramid, a concept of management which is now being challenged in the late sixties and seventies. Decision making centers basically in written policy and centralization of authority, and power is maintained whenever possible.

There is, of course, a distinct reason for this kind of organization—*it produces efficiency.* The bureaucratic pyramid did not drop from the sky, nor was it the creation of some diabolic mind seeking to design a superstate. It resulted primarily from the administrative studies of Frederick Taylor and others, shortly after the turn of the century, when the

Industrial Revolution began to require organizational components to sustain and implement its patterns in society. Through the use of technical qualifications, necessary skills, tenure, and seniority, the system also protects employees against arbitrary dismissal.

PROMOTION BASED ON COMPETENCE

There is an increasing tension, in the system, between the emphasis of organized labor and the concern of management to advance the worker whose performance is most satisfactory and productive for the company. Christian organizations such as colleges have succumbed to the system. We all verbalize that the primary task of a college is teaching, but at the same time we all know that it is the administrator who draws the higher salary. A good public-relations director who knows how to handle the niceties of fund raising will invariably be more richly rewarded by his organization (secular or Christian) than a classroom teacher who may have spent two or three times as many years in preparation for his task and, supposedly, is most directly concerned with the purposes of the organization.

IMPERSONALITY IN EMPLOYEE RELATIONS

In a bureaucracy, the ideal official conducts his office in a spirit of formalistic detachment. I remember being told, in a class in pastoral duties, that the minister should not invite members of the congregation to his home unless he is prepared to set up a system of total equality, lest someone be offended by being left out. Even the terms that we use, such as *Reverend* and *minister*, impress upon our people that great gulf which is fixed between pulpit and pew, between the learned and the laity. (See chapters 1-3 for a discussion of the biblical description of leadership.)

RATIONALITY

Argyris argues that essential rationality is "the most basic property of formal organization." The point is that a bureaucracy has become what it is because of its clear-cut, logical planning processes. There is a constant assumption that the organization behaves rationally. This was never more clearly visible to the national eye than during the Watergate hearings of 1973. What appeared as perfect rationality to the "organization men" of the administration, seemed highly irrational to many viewers.

BUREAUCRACY AND BIBLICAL LEADERSHIP

So what does all of this have to do with a Christian organization? First of all, it must be recognized that bureaucracy is not the horrible specter of demonic control it is often conceived to be. In a discussion, a pastor friend of mine indicated that the church was "becoming too bureaucratic," and that that was one of its major problems. I asked him if he had ever read anything which attempted to deal with bureaucracy in a theological context, and his response was that he had never read *anything* about bureaucracy at all. It is one of those convenient words that we have learned to use when we want to speak out against something that is too big for us to understand, much less to handle.

As a matter of fact, bureaucracy is necessary in a democratic society and in a democratic organization. It is not *bureaucracy* that gives us the trouble, but rather the misuse and abuse of bureaucracy to the point that it becomes a hindrance rather than a help in our organizations. Bureaucracy, like many other tools of accomplishment, makes the proverbial good servant but bad master.

Contrary to popular notions, bureaucracy can be very efficient and an almost necessary tool to productivity. Blau suggests that the term describes a "type of organization designed to accomplish large-scale administrative tasks by systematically coordinating the work of many individuals."[3]

So it is not bureaucracy that causes our problems. It is, rather, a misunderstanding of its inherent evils as well as its helpfulness which leads us astray. It occurred to me, then, that our study might best take the form of pitting bureaucracy, as described in the first section of this chapter, against several concepts which are generally considered contrary to it, in order to see the tension created when bureaucratic concentration of power destroys democratic processes.

BUREAUCRACY VERSUS A "PROFESSIONAL" VIEW OF WORK

The word *professional* appears in quotation marks, because it is a technical term when used in the jargon of management science. Studies by Corwin, in the *Educational Administration Quarterly,* indicate a distinction between the behavior of what Corwin calls "a bureaucratic person" and that of "a professional person." It is not exactly a contrasting relationship, but there are some differences between the outlooks toward the whole matter of the employee's relationship to his institution.

To be more bureaucratic does not necessarily mean to be less professional. The same person could be oriented toward both bureaucratic and professional goals, but the double orientation would necessitate a constant struggle to bring together two things which tend to polarize themselves. A "professional" person in administration tends to emphasize individuals, research, freedom of relationships, skill development through training (rather than practice), decentralization of decision making, and sanctions by a given leader, rather than the constant serving of organizational goals.

Corwin would argue that administrators in a college tend to be more bureaucratic (serve the organization), whereas faculty tend to be more professional (serve their academic disciplines). It should be easy for us to understand that a person serving his academic discipline can also serve the organization, and if he is a Christian, he should serve Christ above either.

On the other hand, it is interesting to notice how often a

professional faculty member becomes a bureaucratic administrator when appointed to a post as dean or, in some large universities, department chairman. Then there is the professional pastor whose prior concerns have always been for the autonomy of the local congregation. Now, as a district superintendent, he seems always to serve the goals and interests of the denomination, sometimes, it may seem, even to the lessening of emphasis on individual congregations within his sphere of authority.

BUREAUCRACY VERSUS EFFECTIVENESS

All of the research done on the subject of bureaucracy tends to conclude that the purely bureaucratic administrative structure is, from a technical point of view, capable of attaining the highest degree of efficiency. Of course, efficiency is measured in terms of product output and the achievement of the goals of the organization.

It is at this point that the concepts of Peter Drucker help us. He candidly offers a marked distinction between *efficiency* and *effectiveness* by suggesting that the former is the ability to do things right, whereas the latter is the ability to do the right things. Drucker pinpoints what he calls five practices, or habits, of the effective executive:

1. Effective executives know where their time goes.
2. Effective executives focus on outward contribution.
3. Effective executives build on strengths.
4. Effective executives concentrate on the few major areas where superior performance will produce outstanding results.
5. Effective executives make effective decisions.[4]

It should not be difficult to note that bureaucracy tends to emphasize *efficiency,* because it focuses on doing things right (task specialization, standardization, etc.), but *effectiveness* is much more concerned with achievement than with process.

BUREAUCRACY VERSUS A DEMOCRATIC VIEW OF ORGANIZATION

There are profound implications in a comparison of bureaucracy with democracy in organizational structure, since bureaucracy is primarily concerned with the systemization of the process of how one's own work fits together with the work of others. Blau's first chapter in *Bureaucracy in Modern Society* identifies three types of association, all of which are to some degree descriptive of the church and every other kind of Christian organization.

1. *The association which exists to produce certain end products and which, therefore, must concern itself with efficiency (doing things right).* Think about your church for just a moment. People who come together in the association that we call *congregation* do not actually create products, but their service to those not in the organization (the witness to the pagan culture and the outreach of world mission) is equivalent to the marketing of an industrial concern. We might also argue that the matter of "doing the right things" is important to the Christian if there are, indeed, biblical absolutes which define the way in which at least some of the work should be done in any age and place.

2. *The association which is established for the purpose of finding intrinsic satisfaction in common activities.* Here efficiency is less relevant, since the members in association are finding the end result of their togetherness in their relationship to each other. This we would call *koinonia* and think of as both an end and a means to an end (cf. chapter 3). Note that bureaucracy is important here, as well, since bureaucracy has to do with the process of how one's work fits together with the work of others.

3. *The association which exists for the purpose of deciding upon common goals and courses of actions.* Surely this also describes the church. To the extent that it has a job to do and a right way to do it, the church must of necessity be a bureaucratic organization. To the extent that the kind of leadership defined for the church in the New Testament (see

chapter 1) is essentially democratic when based on the concept of the universal priesthood of believers, the church must
resist bureaucratization.

BUREAUCRACY VERSUS A CHRISTIAN VIEW OF SOCIETY

In his famous book, *The Lonely Crowd,* David Riesman delineates three periods in the development of any culture: the
high growth potential period, characterized by tradition-
direction; the transitional growth period, characterized by
inner-direction; and the incipient decline of population, characterized by other-direction. The essential point of the book
is that American society in the last half of the twentieth century is living in the "other-directed" period. Therefore the
responsibility of the culture is to preserve individualism in
the face of mass standardization.

Riesman suggests, "In large and bureaucratized organizations people's attention is focused more on products (whether
these are goods, decisions, reports, or discoveries makes little difference) and less on the human element."[5] In this particular section of the book, Riesman is talking about the economic and industrial orientation of an inner-directed society.
His obvious point is the overemphasis on efficiency. However, in discussing the matter of what he calls "the parental
role in the stage of other-direction," Riesman argues, with
Blau, that overbureaucratizing stifles the individuality that
people in the other-directed phase of society claim they
want so desperately.

The implication for the administrator in the Christian organization is that he should focus on the real issue of drawing
out the work of the individual in a genuine way rather than
glossing over the whole situation with some thin veneer of
plastic "human relationism."

When he pours Riesman's theories through the sieve of
special revelation, the evangelical Christian leader finds himself committed to a direction of children in the home, parish-
ioners in the church, and students in the school. This direc-

tion receives its impetus from a power outside and beyond the administrative leadership in each of those organizations, and not merely from some kind of psychological gyroscope which is set into operation by the mature members of society.

BUREAUCRACY VERSUS A BIBLICAL VIEW OF MAN

Let us stay with Riesman just a moment longer. One's philosophy of anything always grows out of his theology, even if he does not admit to having any theology. This is notably true in education, and quite obviously, therefore, in the ministry of many Christian organizations, including the church. If one considers the social system to be in constant flux (which it certainly is, in Western culture), one is tempted to buy the presupposition of most secular psychologists and sociologists that the nature of man is therefore constantly formed by the environmental factors in that flux.

But the "inner-direction" of which Reisman speaks is not generated from the turbulent waters of the social system itself. It arises, rather, from moving and controlling the hearts of Christians, both individually and collectively, so that their work, in the process of association, transcends the norms and standards of society rather than constantly being formed and controlled by them. Living according to absolutes in a relativistic cultural system is not easy, but it is definitely necessary for the church. It always has been, and always will be.

BUREAUCRACY AND INNOVATION

One of the most significant themes of the evangelical church in the early seventies has been its emphasis on renewal. Unfortunately, the term can denote everything from radical restructuring to internal, spiritual revival. No treatment of the matter of structural bureaucracy would be complete without some brief consideration of the relationship between bureaucracy and the process of innovation, creativity, and organizational renewal.

INGREDIENTS OF INNOVATION

There are basic conditions for innovation which must be present in an organization before it can successfully "pull off" structural renewal. It is quite impossible to stuff innovation into an organization from the top of the pyramid, because diversity of input is needed for the creative generation of ideas. Such creativity is not usually born of blind commitment to the organization in its traditional form. It is also never generated by complete alienation from the organization.

As a seminary professor and a churchman, I find myself living in a constant state of tension. With one foot in the church, I share the generally traditional views of other churchmen with respect to the perpetuation of the institutional church. (I do not use these terms negatively.) On the other hand, I spend most of my time in the classroom, where students, very sensitive to the need for structural change, are on the threshold of alienation from existing establishments. I find myself reaching out as far as I can stretch my arms, attempting to pull hands together so that the creativity and innovation we say we want in the church can be made possible by the collective efforts of those who represent both commitment to and criticism of the organization. One feels drawn to the sign which caught President Nixon's attention during his 1968 campaign: "Bring us together."

What, then, are the requirements for structural change? Without attempting to be exhaustive, and working on the assumption that each of the following is self-explanatory, let me list several characteristics of the organization open to creativity and innovation:

1. Structural flexibility, with less emphasis on tight definitions of duties and responsibilities
2. Free and open communications, both up and down the chain of command

3. A break-up of the highly stratified levels of authority (decentralization of power)
4. Replacement of extrinsic rewards of positional status with the intrinsic rewards of institutional involvement in *koinonia*
5. Wider use of group processes, in both small and large groups
6. A lessening of peer competition and political power-play
7. A definitive return to biblical patterns of church process and ministry

FOUR THREATS TO BUREAUCRACY

In a *Think* article entitled "The Coming Death of Bureaucracy," Warren Bennis identifies what he calls "four relevant threats to bureaucracy."[6] His intention is to demonstrate how the process of the modern industrialized society must eventually bring about the death of bureaucracy and produce a new organizational form for the future.

1. *Rapid and unexpected change.* Bureaucracy's strength rests largely in its capacity to manage routine and predict events which it must face. Its chain of command, rules and rigidities, and rationality tend to resist change rather than produce it.

2. *Growth to such size that the volume of an organization's traditional activities is not enough to sustain growth.* The whole idea of conglomerates may have hopelessly overloaded the pyramid, since bureaucracy rests on the ability of the organization to control all of its outgrowths. For instance, a corporation like Standard Oil of New Jersey, with its over one hundred foreign affiliates, may have pulled itself under water in trying to swim too far.

3. *Complexity of modern technology, which makes integration of activities and persons possible without an unusually specialized competence.* It is not only a matter of putting people out of jobs because of mass industrialization and technology, it is also the forcing of masses of people into

meaningless tasks. The other side of the same coin is the great demand for highly trained specialists, who become technicrats. Even with four years of highly specific training, it is possible for a graduate to seek a market which no longer exists because of the acceleration of change.

4. *A psychological threat springing from a change in managerial behavior.* The bureaucratic organization is changing. It is being humanized both in secular industry and in the church. As the focus on human relations becomes more fixed, the organization must face a new concept of management, a new concept of power, and a new concept of organizational values. It is most interesting, for our purposes, to remember that William James linked this kind of thing to religion many years ago, when he coveted "an assurance of safety and a temperate peace, and in relation to others, a preponderance of loving affections." People are now trying to find in their organizations the precise kind of community which the New Testament claims they can and should find in the church.

AUTHORITY IN AN ANTIESTABLISHMENT CULTURE

I have frequently said that the New Testament does not support a leadership concept which is based on authoritarian attitude. Blau argues that the whole concept of authoritarian administration refers to a relationship between persons, and not to an attribute of one individual. It involves exercise of social control which rests on subordinates' willing compliance with certain directives from the superior.

The dilemma of bureaucratic authority, therefore, is that it rests on the power of sanctions (enforced controls) but is weakened by frequently having to use its sanctions to strengthen its authority. Consider, for example, a dean of students in a small Christian college. He wants to maintain a warm climate of rapport so that he can be a friend and confidant to the students in counseling situations. But he is hired to maintain discipline as well, and his authority rests on the sanctions he can impose upon violators. The more he must appeal to this authority, the less attractive he will be for personal counseling.

In a most helpful article on authority in the church, Bill Patterson points out the significance of the difference between human authority and divine authority, a recognition which forces an accompanying commitment to the limitation of objective authority in the church.

> No mere human being—be he elder, deacon, preacher, teacher, editor, professor or somebody's archbishop, cardinal, or pope—has any true religious legislative authority. Some operate as if they do have, as they attempt to change or even deny God's holy word or force their opinion upon others, but God is not mocked, and when His authority is usurped, let that usurping man or system remember that "whatsoever a man soweth, that shall he also reap."[7]

Patterson identifies two extremes polarizing the abuse of power in the church. The extreme to the right is dictatorial, despotic, tyrannical, and coercively authoritarian; the extreme to the left is raw individualism and anarchy.

Once again, the practice of decentralized and participatory democracy, centering in the body and resting upon the principles of universal priesthood, emerges as the only valid New Testament concept of leadership and administration.

One of the most exciting chapters in Alvin Toffler's *Future Shock* is the one in which he discusses what he calls "the coming ad-hocracy." After concurring with Bennis' predictions of the breakup of the pyramid and the demise of bureaucracy, Toffler tries to identify the administrator of the future.

> Executives and managers in this system will function as coordinators between the various transient work teams. They will be skilled in understanding the jargon of different groups of specialists, and they will communicate across groups, translating and interpreting the language of one into the language of another.

Thus we find the emergence of a new kind of organization man—a man who, despite his many affiliations, remains basically uncommitted to any organization. He is willing to employ his skills and creative energies to solve problems with equipment provided by the organization, and within temporary groups established by it. But he does so only so long as the problems interest *him*. He is committed to his own career, and his own self-fulfillment.[8]

Such a picture may or may not be an accurate projection of the future in secular business and industry, but the church must once again avoid the problems of extreme reactionism. Increasing flexibility, yes. Decentralization of authority and decision making, yes. But a situation in which all administrators work for themselves and turn their backs on institutionalized organizations, no. The old maxim calls for moderation in all things; we must be temperate in our knifing of bureaucracy and our welcoming of "ad-hocracy."

6

Christian Implications of the Human-Relations Movement

THE HISTORY of the science of administration can be analyzed from numerous perspectives. But perhaps none is so helpful as a review of the field's self-concept during the first three quarters of the twentieth century. In the interest of brevity, these paragraphs will, of necessity, contain oversimplifications and overgeneralizations, though it might be helpful for the beginning student of administrative science to see where the field has been since its inception about the turn of the century.

From approximately 1900 to 1925, the study of administration focused upon *scientific management* and was characterized by time and motion studies. Sometimes this is referred to as "the efficiency era," and it was marked by the thinking and writing of Calahan and Taylor. Frederick Taylor was an efficiency expert concerned with the development of scientific management in education. There was still very little concern for the role of the individual in the organization and its total administrative process.

In the second quarter of the century, the human relations emphasis spread like fallout over the study of administrative science. The precipitating bomb was the Hawthorne studies, which we will look at in just a moment. Of course, the cue for progress still came from industrial management, although in education, the progressive movement was beginning to demand more of an empirical study of the process of educational administration.

Elton Mayo was the outstanding voice of the human relations movement, as evidenced particularly in his book, *The Human Problems of an Industrial Civilization,* published in 1933. This book clearly indicates Mayo's debt to both Freud and Janet, as psychology began to make its impact on the study of management. According to Mayo, "The chief difficulty of our time is the breakdown of the social codes that formerly disciplined us to effective working together." He argues further, "We have too few administrators alert to the fact that it is a human social and not an economic problem which they face."[1] The result of the Hawthorne studies was a classic swing of the pendulum away from an *emphasis on efficiency and product output* to an extreme *emphasis on the role of the worker* in the organization.

The emphasis for the past twenty or twenty-five years has been on the construction of a theoretical approach to administration. In the early fifties, there was revived interest in the "trait approach," in an attempt to emphasize which personality characteristics blend to make a good administrator. Another angle was the "three-ingredient approach" to a study of administration, focusing on the task, the man, and the setting. Behavioral change was not properly considered during the fifties, and the relationship of variable factors was overlooked. What resulted was largely a taxonomy of administrative characteristics. The genuinely theoretical approach tends to look at its subject matter as a system, and is therefore sometimes referred to as the "systems approach." It harks back to the old axiom, "The whole is greater than the sum of its parts," and asks questions about the relationships between the parts of organizations, on the assumption that each part affects the others.

In the past ten years or so, the field has been turning more toward empirical research and practical application. It seems to me that since administration is a single science (an axiom believed by most professionals working in the academic side of the field), a principle approach is most valid. Sometimes people complain about such an approach being impractical, but John Dewey was right when he once indicated that there is nothing as practical as a good theory.

If Christian leaders and administrators can learn the basic principles of management science which have emerged from this seventy-five-year history, run those principles through what I have often called the "funnel of biblical revelation," and then apply them flexibly to varying kinds of administrative tasks and situations, we can begin to see a renewal of leadership and administration in the work of churches and Christian organizations.

THE IMPACT OF THE HAWTHORNE STUDIES

Fifty years ago, the Massachusetts Institute of Technology conducted a series of studies at the Hawthorne plant of the Western Electric Company, located in Chicago. The studies lasted from 1924 until 1932, and concentrated in testing the production of a selected group of workers under varying conditions.

In the first series of tests, the investigators varied the lighting in three different parts of the plant, with the result that production levels were always higher at the end of the test than at the beginning. Furthermore, the levels did *not* fall off when the lighting was finally decreased. Such results were perplexing, so procedures were modified in a second series of tests, which utilized the comparable-groups technique. An attempt was made to control as many sources of variation as possible by placing together the groups showing an appreciable production increase of almost the same magnitude.

The third series of tests coupled the comparable-groups technique with a decrease instead of an increase of illumination. More complicated test theories were designed, focusing on shortening the working day, lengthening the morning rest period, offering special refreshments, and other changes calculated to measure the environmental influences on output. Invariably, what happened was that in the experiments, the investigators were faced with results that should not have happened if their presuppositions were accurate. In their confusion, they tried to eliminate the ambiguity instead of understanding it. Mayo writes:

> The Western Electric experiment was primarily directed not to the external condition but to the internal organization. By strengthening the "temperamental" inner equilibrium of the workers, the company enabled them to achieve a mental "steady state" which offered a high resistance to a variety of external conditions.[2]

Of course, Mayo's analysis here was offered late in the process, after the investigators discovered that it was *not* the impersonal, mechanical, and environmental factors that were most influential in affecting the production rate. Rather, it was the fact that *for the first time in their careers, these workers were given special attention by a group of people who seemed genuinely interested in them,* even if that interest existed primarily for the ultimate benefit of the organization!

F. J. Roethlisberger, some years later, refers to the whole experiment as "the systematic exploitation of the simple and the obvious." The "simple and the obvious" is the conclusion that people will work harder and better when someone is paying attention to them on a personal level. The human relations era in management science had been born.

"HAWTHORNE EFFECT"

One of the interesting by-products of the Hawthorne experiments was the gift to socio-psychological literature of a new term, *Hawthorne effect.* This might be defined as *a change in a worker's productivity brought about by the change in the social interaction of the work area.* At least, that is a primary definition. In a much broader sense, the term is now used to describe any kind of variable, in the process of research, over which the researcher does not have control. Said variable may account for behavioral changes which were not brought about by control procedures which he designed.

Perhaps a simple illustration is in order here. Suppose I give my seminary students a test carefully calculated to measure their ability to perform a certain task (let us say a teaching practicum in an adult class at a nearby church). Seven students are teaching seven controlled classes, and in the experiment, we are attempting to also control as many environmental and other variables as we can. But without thinking, my wife and I invite one of the students and his wife to our home for dinner on a Saturday evening before he is to teach one of the experimental sessions.

In four or five hours of interaction that evening, we carefully avoid the subject of his teaching, lest somehow we corrupt the validity of comparison between his work and the the work of his peers. But an affinity develops between us which spurs that student on to unusual efforts in his teaching throughout the whole project. The result of his work, therefore, is to be accounted for not by any of the carefully conducted procedures to which we had all agreed, but rather by an interpersonal contact with his professor which none of the other workers had experienced. That contact becomes a "Hawthorne effect" in the research.

At Hawthorne, the workers were obtaining psychological satisfaction from new patterns of interaction which placed them in special positions as the subjects of the experiments. Amitai Etzioni says, "The discovery of the significance of 'social factors' was to become the major finding of the Hawthorne studies."[3]

When the Hawthorne investigators discovered the situation, they could very well have closed shop with the comfort that they had at least contributed a new term to the English language. Some did. But others kept trying to control the variables to obtain additional answers to the questions which had originally been raised in the experiments. Some of the researchers put aside experimental designs and focused on an analysis of the roles in which the workers were engaged beneath the surface. Though plagued by ambiguity and inconclusive results, they dared push on to provide a foundation which became instrumental in the development of an understanding of counselor-counselee roles in organizational human relations.

For example, they began to understand that human problems were a big factor in the work pattern, and that the requirements of the individual and of the organization must in some way be kept in balance (see chap. 10). But how do we determine the requirements of the individual? The investigators (now called counselors) soon learned that individuals did not themselves understand what they were trying to do, and consequently would not openly discuss their problems. By remaining aloof from role adoption themselves, and disassociating their function from any other normal function performed in the work area, the counselors learned that *interaction was the important element in the human relations process.*

The results of this important research were published by Dickson and Roethlisberger in 1966, under the title *Counseling in an Organization.* I have already referred, in chapter four, to one of the key findings described in the book, namely the identification of the *sources* of employee concern and the five basic concerns of employees. According to the authors,

> Any counselor who has become dedicated to his catalytic role, wherein the process of trying to describe it in chapter XI, it will be remembered, words failed us, becomes almost by definition anti-labeling, anti-classification, anti-problem, anti-evaluation, anti-typological, etc. Why? Because these intellectual processes and their products can become so easily instruments of misevaluation instead of for dynamic openness. They deny man's existential condition, that he unfortunately exists before he knows what he can become,

for man's becomingness there are no answers at the end of the book. Process is all; substance is illusion. So it is not strange that many "good counselors" often tend to become kinds of mystics (remember, we are using this word descriptively and not evaluatively) who eschew substantive knowledge about human behavior and wisely, perhaps, do not write books about it.[4]

A Christian Analysis of the Human-Relations Thrust

Perhaps there might be some merit in first suggesting what I am *not* attempting to do in this section of the chapter. It is not my intent to "Christianize" the research of Mayo, Roethlisberger, Dickson, and others. But since virtually no research is being done in administration in the Christian organization, and since administration *is* a single science, it is only reasonable that those of us who are interested in applying the findings of industrial and business management research to our work in the church, mission organizations, Christian schools, and other kinds of Christian organizations will learn to study the findings of secular administrative science with a carefully trained, theological eye.

To say it one more time, we will learn to pour all information we find through the funnel of special revelation to see what comes out at the other end for our use. So, without a great deal of theological jargon or hermeneutical fanfare, let me draw some conclusions in the form of principles which I have found coming out of my funnel of late.

Human relations is both a means and an end

The purpose of human relations in secular business can be very clearly stated: Human relations is a tool, or means, for the achievement of the company's goals. Much of the literature in management science warns business executives to avoid the dangers of making human relations an end instead of a means. For example, when elimination of conflict becomes a primary goal of the organization; when an individual's expectations conflict with the organizational goals; when human relations efforts center only on therapy, with no contribution to the organization's goals; or when human relations becomes a substitute for higher-level action, it is argued that human relations has gotten out of hand. The tool has become an end in itself rather than the means which it must be.

But although the church is an organization, it is more than an organization; it is an organism. And as an organism, it surely recognizes that one of its biblical imperatives is the creation of the atmosphere of unity and community described in chapter three. The very process of the functioning of the body is the relationship of people to one another, and the achievement of the best possible harmony and spiritual vitality in that relationship is one of the goals of the church.

To be more specific, loving each other, bearing each other's burdens, and putting each other before ourselves, are ends to be sought. As these ends are sought, however, they also become a means of evangelism as an unbelieving world looks in, sees the love, and wonders about the Christ who can produce it (John 13). Herein lies Schaeffer's "ultimate apologetic," with its emphasis on love and unity in the body.

MANIPULATION OF PEOPLE IS WRONG

When human relations is viewed as a means, it can be abused to the point where it becomes a tool in the hands of a totalitarian administration using it to bludgeon the workers into conformity with the organization's standards. Perhaps *bludgeon* is a poor choice of a word here, because the very nature of the tool implies a soft handling of people. Christians should be properly frightened by what they read in such books as B. F. Skinner's *Beyond Freedom and Dignity*. The necessity of abject control of people in order to achieve some purpose desirable to the controller is manipulation of the first rank.

Over twenty years ago, Skinner was stating:

the hypothesis that man is not free is essential to the application of scientific methods of the study of human behavior. The free inner man who is held responsible for his behavior . . . is only a pre-scientific substitute for the kinds of causes which are discovered in the course of scientific analysis. All these alternative causes lie outside the individual.[5]

In stark contrast to Skinner's animalistic behaviorism, the Bible teaches that the Christian man is free and dare not sell his soul to anything other than the lordship of Christ in his life (1 Co 6:12). Because of his high view of man as an image (marred by sin but restored in Christ), the Christian leader tends to value man as a self-actualizing personality. He values creativity and wants to discover and maintain the conditions which encourage rather than impede the self-actualization process, and to set up these conditions with a minimum of power control. Although not all of the concepts of Carl Rogers will coincide with biblical Christianity, he stands in positive contrast to Skinner with respect to his view of man:

We can choose to use our growing knowledge to enslave people in ways never dreamed of before, depersonalizing them, controlling them by means so carefully selected that they will perhaps never be aware of their loss of personhood. We can choose to utilize our scientific knowledge to make men necessarily happy, well behaved, and productive, as Dr. Skinner suggests. We can, if we wish, choose to make men submissive, conforming, docile. Or at the other end of the spectrum of choice we can choose to use the behavioral sciences in ways which will free, not control; which will bring about constructive variability, not conformity; which will develop creativity, not contentment; which will facilitate each person in his self-directed process of becoming; which will aid individuals, groups, and even the concepts of science to become self-transcending in freshly adaptive ways of meeting life and its problems.[6]

INTERACTION IS BASIC TO THE HUMAN-RELATIONS PROCESS

At this point, the Christian finds himself in wholehearted agreement with the research of the Hawthorne studies. In formal or informal interaction between counselor and counselee, through daily contact with workers as a group, the strategic nature of interpersonal communications cannot be overemphasized.[7] It is my contention that the pastor's primary role is that of proclamation and exposition—he is God's prophet and God's teacher. But in the role of prophet and teacher, he must also remember his social functions and the effect of his verbal and nonverbal behavior in the process of interaction.

The Sunday school superintendent would do well to follow Mayo's suggestion to strengthen the "temperamental inner equilibrium of the workers." Better curriculum is to be applauded and well-equipped classrooms are only a necessary part of the job. But adding all of these and a host of other external improvements is like increasing the lighting at the Hawthorne plant. What counts, in the final analysis, is that superintendent's relationship to his departmental superintendents and to his teachers.

BOTH THE ORGANIZATION AND THE WORKER MUST BE CHANGED

The overwhelming bulk of the literature on the human relations movement emphasizes the changing of the organization to better meet the needs of the worker. How interesting it is that the clamor of early industrial civilization fifty years ago is now being renewed in antiestablishment concerns of the 1970s. And now, as then, an overemphasis on *changing the organization* (as needed as this surely is) tends to minimize the importance of *changing the worker.* I am not talking about the rank conditioning kind of change which Skinner and his associates advocate. I am, rather, thinking of the kind of inner change which comes, according to Rogers, through the self-actualizing process of nondirective counseling. In the view of the Christian, that change comes through the supernatural work of the Holy Spirit utilizing the power and dynamic of God's revelation to develop a steady and progressive maturity in the life of the Christian. This maturity affects not only the spiritual dimensions of his life, but every aspect of his relationships to things and people (Eph 4:17-32).

In his most helpful book, *Modern Organizations*, Amitai Etzioni grapples with many of the problems that I am mentioning in this book. The question that he does *not* raise, however, and therefore does not answer, is whether a constant determination to change the organization (whether for its own good or for the good of the worker) is the best way to approach the problem of the harmonious synthesis of organizational structure and personality structure. He does not overtly consider the possibility of changing the worker. For example, in dealing with the matter of authority, Etzioni suggests:

> The ultimate source of the organizational dilemmas viewed up to this point is the incomplete matching of the personalities of the participants with their organizational roles. If personalities could be shaped to fit specific organizational roles, or organizational roles to fit specific personalities, many of the pressures to displace goals, much of the need to control performance and a good part of the alienation would disappear.[8]

After seeing the above words, the reader's eyes begin to sparkle and his mind moves forward in anticipation, only to find Etzioni suggesting again that personality shaping and role matching are virtually impossible. Thus, with one sweep of the pen, we clear the slate of the possibility of changing men and go back to changing the organization.

But the Christian closes Etzioni and opens Ephesians, where he reads in chapter four such concepts as "equipping

of the saints"; "building up of the body"; "attaining the unity
of the faith"; "speaking the truth in love"; "growing up . . .
into him"; "being fitted and held together"; and "affirming
together with the Lord." Verses 20-24 of that chapter contrast the old, pagan ways with the process of becoming in
Christ:

> But you did not learn Christ in this way, if indeed you have
> heard Him, and have been taught in Him, just as truth is in
> Jesus, that, in reference to your former manner of life, you
> lay aside the old self, which is being corrupted in accordance
> with the lusts of deceit, and that you be renewed in the
> spirit of your mind, and put on the new self, which in the
> likeness of God has been created in righteousness and holi-
> ness of the truth [NASB].

THE CONCEPT OF LATENT ROLES DESERVES OUR ATTENTION

A part of the findings of the Hawthorne study has to do
with an understanding of the characteristics of latent roles in
the organization. Most individuals in an organization are involved in a variety of interpersonal relationships, the working group being only one of them. Each person, therefore,
plays many roles as they fit into his numerous activities. It
is obvious that one individual cannot play all his roles at the
same time, so he plays roles that match the situation in which
he happens to be. The ones which he is not using at any
given moment are referred to as latent roles.

Latent role characteristics are such that they lend themselves to improving human problems when they are used
properly by a trained counselor and related to the process of
interaction. Part of the difficulty is that the individual tends
to be confused by his roles and frequently is ambiguous about
which one to use at which time.

Because the individual wants to be recognized for what he
is and for what he can become, he uses latent roles to help
fulfill these higher-order needs. He does not want to become
submerged in organizational regulations and red tape. He

does not want to be lost in the bureaucracy and have his process of self-actualization stifled.

America learned in 1964 that university students do not like to be treated like computer cards. The original Berkeley revolt was not a political struggle but a reaction against depersonalization in contemporary educational processes. When a Berkeley student turned radical revolutionary, his role as a student became latent.

We must not confuse a latent role with a deviant role. A deviant tends to be against everything and wants the world to do things his way. The latent-role player is reacting against being pressured into conformity by the overwhelming power of his organization.

The Christian answer is again one of freedom and joy. It is a process of changing the organization into a people-centered, caring *koinonia*, while at the same time helping people to be less reactionary because they are growing and maturing in Christ (Col 2:4-8).

The responsibility of the administrator goes even a step beyond what God expects of all Christians. The leader must appreciate and recognize other people as unique, relate to groups well, and structure an environment in which these goals are attainable for other people. In short, he must establish a human-relations climate as the norm for his organization, and set the tone for the implementation of interpersonal relations and communications in that organization.

7

A Christian Analysis of Motivation Theory

IF IT IS TRUE that all employers must understand human behavior and personnel motivation, then it is certainly of great importance that those of us who work constantly with volunteer employees have a clear grasp of the dynamics that operate within an organization to achieve a high level of motivation. Yet many church leaders and administrators in other Christian organizations have not taken the time or the effort to explore the interesting and helpful research which has been carried out in industrial management science with respect to the issues of motivation and persuasion.

Perhaps no area of management research has been given more attention than motivation theory, unless it be the matter of individual versus institutional dynamic (discussed in chapter ten). One of the most significant findings which came out of the Hawthorne studies is the apparent priority of nonmonetary factors in the job. Management has discovered that employees do not work better or maintain high levels of loyalty to companies just because they are given more money or better fringe benefits.

Because the whole matter of employee motivation is so strategically related to human behavior, the discipline of psychology has given us the most helpful insights into this crucial field of study. Dr. Mungo Miller, the president of Affiliated Psychological Services, suggests six general principles which psychologists have studied in their research on motivation:

1. Motivation is psychological, not logical. It is primarily an emotional process.
2. Motivation is fundamentally an unconscious process. The behavior we see in ourselves and others may appear to be illogical, but somehow, inside the individual, what he is doing makes sense to him.
3. Motivation is an individual matter. The key to a person's behavior lies within himself.
4. Not only do motivating needs differ from person to person, but in any individual, they vary from time to time.
5. Motivation is inevitably a social process. We must depend on others for satisfaction of many of our needs.
6. In the vast majority of our daily actions, we are guarded by habits established by motivational processes that were active many years earlier.[1]

In my larger book on leadership, I have suggested that phenomenological psychology, with its self-concept theory, seems to come the closest to a Christian analysis of the nature and behavior of man. Its emphasis is on the internal view which man has of himself, and how he sees himself in relation to others and the work task. It offers, in my judgment, a pleasant contrast to the animalism of the Skinnerian behavioristic theory. It is interesting that most of the management psychologists who have explored motivation generally fall within the phenomenological camp.

Jesus once said, that it is not that which man puts into his mouth that is destructive, but rather that which comes out, because it indicates the kind of inner nature he possesses (Mt 15:11, 18-20). In the book of Proverbs we read "as [a man] thinketh in his heart, so is he" (Pr 23:7). This is not to baptize phenomenological psychology in a few proof texts and call it "Christian." It is rather to say that *a psychological*

position which emphasizes the importance of the inner na-
ture of man is certainly more within the realm of Christian
theism than one which emphasizes a behavior which results
only from mechanistic, environmental forces.

ROKEACH RESEARCH: FIVE BELIEF SYSTEMS

One of the most interesting studies of inner motivation
with respect to purchasing has been carried out by Dr. Milton Rokeach, a professor of psychology at Michigan State
University in East Lansing. The research was initially reported at an advertising convention, in a speech entitled
"Images of the Consumer's Changing Mind on and off Madison Avenue." In it, Rokeach explores "the different kinds of
beliefs which all men have" and asks, "How easily is one kind
changed compared with another kind?"[2]

Although the address is clearly slanted toward the matter
of changing a person's viewpoints about product purchasing,
some of the implications are most remarkable for their strategic relationship to what we might call developing convic-
tions or building a Christian value system in children, youth,
and adults in Christian homes and churches.

The major assumption of the research is that all persons
have belief systems (again a commitment to "inner-man"
psychology), and that each belief system contains tens of
thousands of beliefs. Since all of these beliefs and ideas cannot be equally important to the individual, a hierarchy is
constructed attempting to measure the proximity of a given
belief to the core of the system.

Rokeach argues, "We must assume that the more important a belief, the more it will resist change; and the more
trivial a belief, the more easily it can be changed." He ex-
pands the argument to assume that the more important a
belief which is changed, the more widespread the repercus-
sions in the rest of the belief system, because many of the
beliefs hooked up with it will change too.

PRIMITIVE BELIEFS

In the Rokeach hierarchy, a primitive belief is one which a person holds because it attracts a nearly 100% social consensus. Primitive beliefs are fundamental. Almost all the persons we know would agree with them. Consequently, they are the most resistant to change. When primitive beliefs are brought into question, we begin to suspect the rationality of the questioner, or worse, our own rationality.

BELIEFS OF DEEP PERSONAL EXPERIENCE

Such a belief does not depend upon social support or consensus but runs a direct line to some experience which the holder has had. The incontrovertibility of such a belief is based on that experience, and therefore the holder does not consider it consequential whether anyone else accepts it or not. If you saw a twenty-foot-tall pink giraffe while taking a walk, it is not going to impress you that I have never seen the giraffe, nor that I do not believe that you have seen the giraffe. The more realistic the experience, the more unshakable the belief which emerges from it.

Rokeach points out that experiential beliefs may be *positive* or *negative*. When they are negative, we tend to call them *phobias* or *inferiority complexes*. When they are positive, the self-concept convinces us that we are intelligent, rational, and competent people. Quite obviously, experiential beliefs are not always in harmony with reality. I do not care what you say, you did *not* see that twenty-foot pink giraffe! Yet it is possible for you to go through the rest of your life, absolutely convinced that you did, though you may never find another person to agree with you.

BELIEFS OF DEEP PERSONAL EXPERIENCE

AUTHORITY BELIEFS

This is the old, TV quiz-game, "Who Do You Trust?" Obviously, no man can ascertain for himself the truth of all things. Especially in a complex society of knowledge explosion, we find ourselves constantly depending upon the word of others. Does the government tell us the truth about the war? Can your family doctor be trusted when he diagnoses cancer? Does the mechanic really know when your car needs a tune-up?

AUTHORITY BELIEFS

Somehow, we develop beliefs as to which authorities can be trusted and which cannot. Again, these conclusions may often run counter to reality, but anyone who has studied American politics knows that authority beliefs are tenaciously held.

PERIPHERAL BELIEFS

A peripheral belief differs from an authority belief because it is a derivation. Rather than focusing now upon a belief *in my pastor*, I am focusing on a belief in *something I have heard him say.* Do I know that certain kinds of moon rocks have been brought back from lunar expeditions because I have personally been to Houston to study them? Of course

This verse means that we should . . .

PERIPHERAL BELIEFS

not. Even if I were to study them, I would not know whether
they came from the moon, Death Valley, or the Bad Lands of
South Dakota. Since I am not an authority on lunar rocks, I
assume that such authorities are competent and that the information which they give me about moon rocks is accurate.
The belief is called peripheral because I could easily change
my mind about that information if the people in Houston
publish a differing report.

It is at this point that Rokeach offers a couple of sentences
which have profound, theological impact in the area of Christian education:

> Many people adhere to a particular religious or political
> belief system because they identify with a particular author-
> ity. Such peripheral beliefs can be changed providing the
> suggestion for change emanates from one's authority, or pro-
> viding there is a change in one's authority.[3]

INCONSEQUENTIAL BELIEFS

An inconsequential belief is at the bottom of the hierarchy,
or the outer rim of a series of concentric circles. If an inconsequential belief is changed, the total system is basically un-
affected. Do I believe that Chevrolets are better than Fords?

Maybe so, but if someone were to convince me that Plymouths are really better than both, very little in my total value system would change.

Why is this helpful to us in the Christian organization? Simply because so many young people and adults in the evangelical camp seem to maintain beliefs which are floating somewhere between authority and inconsequential. If at any point they lose faith in the authority (such as a pastor or a parent), the entire belief system, with respect to theology and Christian conviction, slides right down the tubes. Not only that, but peripheral beliefs are particularly shaky, since the authority source can shift to a university professor or media hero and leave God's intended sources of authority well behind.

INCONSEQUENTIAL BELIEFS

Obviously, we ought to be striving for a strengthening of authority sources, but that is by no means the best approach. What we *must* do is to somehow *lead our people into significant, first-hand experiences of Christian truth, so that a confrontation with the message of the Word and the ministry of the Holy Spirit becomes not only the source for belief systems, but also the motivating pattern for service to Christ and relationships in the church.*

MASLOW'S HIERARCHY OF HUMAN NEEDS

According to Abraham Maslow, man is a perpetually wanting organism.[4] His wants stem from five basic human needs, of relative predominance. The hierarchy concept stems from Maslow's belief that when a lower need is satisfied, it disappears and is replaced by a higher-order need. Thus, gratification is considered as important a concept, in motivating theory as deprivation, since it releases the individual from dominance by a lower order and enables him to concentrate on more social, or higher-order, needs. Once a need has been satisfied, it is no longer considered a "need," since it exists then only in a potential fashion and may emerge again at any time to dominate the individual. It is the unsatisfied needs which dominate a person and organize his behavior.

The hierarchy of basic human needs, arranged in order from lower to higher, includes the following: physiological needs, safety needs, belongingness and love needs, esteem needs, and the need for self-actualization. Maslow would argue that the order is not fixed (there have been a number of exceptions), but that it nevertheless holds true for the overwhelming majority of persons encountered in his research.

Physiological needs are the issues of subsistence and, consequently, are the most dominant of all. They include such factors as hunger, thirst, and sleepiness. They are relatively independent of each other and of other issues in the motivational process, allowing a person to be completely dominated by a single physiological need, such as hunger.

When the physiological needs are satisfied, safety needs may emerge. It is quite possible that safety needs dominate only in emergencies such as war, disease, and natural catastrophe. When one has been shipwrecked, for example, it does not seem consequential to him that he might also be hungry.

Love, affection, and belongingness needs will emerge if the physiological and safety needs are fairly well gratified. They are demonstrated by a desire for affectionate relations with people in general, and manifested in a longing for group acceptance or group membership.

The next step upward in the hierarchy is the esteem-need level. Satisfaction of this need can be derived from self-respect or self-esteem as a feeling of adequacy accruing from achievements and accomplishments, prestige, status, or appreciation by others.

When all of these lower needs are satisfied, then the need for self-actualization emerges and becomes the significant factor in the motivational process. It represents a longing for self-fulfillment and a desire to become everything that one is capable of becoming.

Once again, an analysis of a secular theoretician in the light of the New Testament offers some striking insights. Surely we understand James to be saying that the communication of Christian theology to a man who is starving is sheer nonsense (Ja 2:14-20). His need for inner peace and eternal salvation is properly recognized by him only when physiological and safety needs have been met.

On the other hand, a company (or a church) does not motivate a man by offering him additional fulfillment of needs that have already been met. When a man has enough bread, he is not impelled to action by the offer of more bread, or even by the potential wherewithal to buy more bread.

What is there about Christian ministry that is self-actualiz-

ing? Is it possible that the discouraged pastor or a Sunday
school teacher ready to quit finds himself in that position because no one has taught him to think of his service as self-
actualizing? Has the Christian-service dropout developed a
distorted, slave-to-the-church concept of his task? Is it possible that the task itself has very little self-actualizing potential?

My brother-in-law tells hilarious stories of the days when
he was a factory worker putting screws in refrigerator doors
all day long—a task hardly calculated to produce self-esteem
or a feeling of belongingness and importance. How are we
helping our people to understand that teaching and leading
in Christian ministry is not the theological equivalent of putting screws in a refrigerator door on some assembly line?

HERZBERG'S MOTIVATION-HYGIENE THEORY

Frederick Herzberg is professor of psychology at Western
Reserve University and has also served as research director
of the Psychological Service of Pittsburg for several years.
Primarily through his orientation toward mental illness and
health theories, he has developed what is called the Motiva-
tion-Hygiene Theory and has detailed it in three books entitled *Job Attitudes: Review of Research and Opinion; The
Motivation to Work;* and *Work and the Nature of Man.*[5] Actually the three volumes represent three stages in the development of the theory. They detail the gathering of scientific inquiry and data, new research and investigation, and
actual construction of the conceptual theory. The interesting outcome of the Herzberg study is that the factors which
make people satisfied with their jobs are *not* the same as
those which make them dissatisfied, nor are these factors
necessarily the opposites of one another.

Herzberg concludes that the presence of so-called satisfiers
tends to increase an individual's satisfaction with his work,
but their absence does not necessarily make a worker dissatisfied, only apathetic. Similarly, the presence of so-called dis-

satisfiers makes people unhappy or disgruntled about their work, but the absence of dissatisfiers does not necessarily make them happy on the job. Here are the lists which came out of the research:[6]

Satisfiers	Dissatisfiers
Achievement	Interpersonal relations (both with superiors and peers)
Recognition	Technical ability of the supervisor
Work itself	Company policy and administration
Responsibility	Working conditions
Advancement	Personal life off of the job

It is interesting to note that the satisfiers distinctly relate to the work itself, whereas the dissatisfiers quite frequently relate to the job context, or the environment out of which the job emerges. Herzberg concludes that the presence of satisfiers leads to higher productivity, but the dissatisfiers, on the other hand, do not necessarily lead to lower productivity. Strauss and Sayles summarize the Herzberg findings well in a brief paragraph:

> The experimenters called the factors which lead to this rather sterile, non-involved attitude "hygienic factors" (since they are used to avoid trouble). We shall accordingly call management which emphasizes these factors "Hygienic Management." Such a "be good" policy may provide a pleasant environment in which to work and a considerable amount of around-the-job satisfaction, but little satisfaction through the job, and little sense of enthusiasm or creativity.[7]

Once again, we can be helped by the work of secular research. The Christian organization needs to emphasize the satisfiers of achievement, responsibility, and advancement.

But surely our primary deficiency does not lie here, but in our failure to recognize the presence of dissatisfiers. The problem develops because we have frequently failed to recognize their existence and have concentrated our attention on multiplying and enhancing the satisfiers, while the dissatisfiers may have been chipping away at the morale, and consequently the motivation, of our workers.

Surely it is thoroughly biblical for a Christian employer to be concerned with the life of his employees off of the job. Surely it is consistent with Christian theology to recognize that the inner factors of a man's attitude toward personnel, himself, and his supervisors will represent a crucial role in his service performance.

ZALEZNIK AND THE INDIVIDUALISTIC VIEW

As I have indicated earlier in this volume, Abraham Zaleznik is one of the few management theoreticians who seeks to place responsibility upon the worker rather than constantly harping on changing the organization. His position emphasizes an internal view of man and attempts to show how men, by the strength of their character and personality, can remake organizations. The effect of their personality induces a contagious desire to perform that is considerably stronger in directing organizations than are depersonalized systems such as interlocking committee structures or shared management. The release of this individual energy and its contagion of desire to perform may well occur within organizational structures, but the impulse and inspiration are derived from individual personality. Zaleznik points out that even when we are interested in group and organizational problems as we should be, the ultimate "chooser," or decision maker, is the individual. Even when he performs within groups, he is still performing as an individual. Since this is the case, it is essential for leadership to understand the ways in which an individual personality is influenced by the attributes of the groups in which he works and lives, the other individuals with whom he interacts, the organization within which he and his group work, and the cultures in which they all live.[8]

The Christian leader will find himself nodding vigorously when he reads Zaleznik's emphasis on individuality starting in family life. Specific persons, and his relationships to them, influence each person and are in turn influenced by him. As his world and self broaden, he is increasingly concerned with the environment beyond his immediate, face-to-face groups.[9]

One of the reasons why Zaleznik's theorizing appeals to me is his concern for changing men rather than organizations. Or perhaps I should say, changing organizations by first changing the individuals which make up those organizations. In these days of enormous emphasis on change in the church, Zaleznik's focus ought to put cautious guidelines on the massive restructuring advocated by some renewal writers. According to Zaleznik, the social scientist who takes such a utopian position (that organizations can consistently be conformed to suit the individuals) only exerts a new type of stress on individuals who still must act within the framework of their own, personal, developmental problems.

Zaleznik also emphasizes that while behavioral scientists like Maslow and Herzberg can be enormously helpful in providing theoretical constructs, the decision as to how to use that information must ultimately fall to the leader in the local organization. What disturbs me, with respect to churches and Christian organizations, is that the information of the behavioral scientists is meaningless unless leaders in those organizations make themselves aware of it, run it through a proper, theological grid, and seek a practical application in local problem-solving. I suppose it is precisely to that end that I am offering these chapters.

McGREGOR: THEORY X AND THEORY Y

This is one of the better motivational theories, which again focuses on individual personality. McGregor argues, "Management has adopted generally a far more humanitarian set of values; it has successfully strived to give more equitable and more generous treatment to employees . . . *but it has done all of these things without changing its fundamental theory of management.*"[10]

The basic assumptions of Theory X, McGregor delineates in this fashion:

1. The average human being has an inherent dislike of work and will avoid it if he can.

2. Because of this human characteristic of dislike of work, most people must be coerced, controlled, directed, threatened with punishment to get them to put forth adequate effort for the achievement of organizational objectives.

3. The average human being prefers to be directed, wishes to avoid responsibility, has relatively little ambition, and wants security above all.[11]

McGregor argues that as long as management holds such presuppositions it can never develop a genuinely human-relations context for work motivation. He refers to Theory Y as "the integration of individual and organizational goals" and offers some basic assumptions in contradistinction to those held by practitioners of Theory X.

1. The expenditure of physical and mental effort in work is as natural as play or rest.

2. External control and the threat of punishment are not the only means for bringing about effort toward organizational objectives. Man will exercise self-direction and self-control in the service of objectives to which he is committed.

3. Commitment to objectives is a function of the rewards associated with their achievement.

4. The average human being learns, under proper conditions, not only to accept but to seek responsibility.

5. The capacity to increase a relatively high degree of imagination, ingenuity, and creativity in the solution of

organizational problems is widely, not narrowly, distributed in the population.

6. Under the conditions of modern industrial life, the intellectual potentialities of the average human being are only partly utilized.[12]

Once again it seems that the alert reader can recognize some basically biblical undertones in the work of McGregor. He suggests, for example, a high view of man rather than the low view so often obvious in old "carrot-and-the-stick" approaches to leadership and administration. He also takes a high view of the nature of work, a position consistent with biblical rubrics as early as the twentieth chapter of Exodus, and perhaps as early as God's activity in creation recorded in the first two chapters of the Old Testament (Gen 1–2). He also recognizes the difficulties in achieving genuinely humane management in the complex democracy in which we all must function today.

Let us look at the end of the whole matter, some meaningful remarks about how to translate helpful theory into the practice of management. Motivation obviously has to do with motive, and motive can be simply defined as that which incites an individual to action, sustains the action, and gives direction to this action once the individual has been initially aroused.

In the *Master Plan of Evangelism,* Robert E. Coleman lists eight aspects of motivation used by Christ with his disciples: selection, association, consecration, giving, demonstration, delegation, supervision, and reproduction.[13] Note the personal emphasis in all of these. Christ's pattern was to build His life into a small number of men rather than to spend the majority of His time speaking impersonally to large numbers of men (Mt 10).

So perhaps first in the matter of translating theory into action, is a *commitment to the discipleship approach in one's relationship to his workers.* That will obviously be more easy to attain in some supervisory situations than in others, but that does not make it any less important.

Another factor is *a significant program of education for all responsible employees.* A pastor should constantly be exposing his men to materials in the behavioral sciences and management research, as well as to what scant materials are available in a theological analysis of the field. Obviously we are talking here about a long-term process rather than a "fixed-point millennium" with respect to either organizational or individual change.

The third ingredient of implementation is the matter of *managing the motivation.* Two aspects of producing motivation seem to outshine all others in importance. First of all, communication must provide thorough information to all personnel. The communication flow should be two-way—down from management and up from the workers. Secondly, mutual agreement upon goals and standards should pervade all organizational processes. We must *know* together and *agree* together what we are going to *do* together.

Another factor is *the participation of as many personnel as can be comfortably handled in one's sphere of control.* We know that change occurs faster and is more lasting when it is accompanied by a high degree of interaction among the workers. This obviously forces an emphasis on people rather than program. It helps us to zero in on the matter of God's design through spiritual gifts, calls, and empowerings. Objectives and needs precede forms.

Above all, we must avoid the common sins of superficial motivation: guilt motivators ("If you are really a loyal church member you will do this"); plastic enthusiasm ("Everything is really great at our church"); and manipulation (using others against their will to obtain your own desired ends.).

8

Patterns of Interpersonal Relations

THE FAMOUS SPANISH PHILOSOPHER, Baruch Spinoza, once said, "Things that have nothing in common with each other cannot be understood by each other mutually; the concept of the one does not include the conception of the other." That is a philosopher's way of stating the basic axiom of human communication; namely, that it is *meaning exchange* rather than *word exchange.*

Communication does not occur in isolation, and it does not have to be verbal. The process of socialization within an organization takes place primarily through interpersonal communications, even when the communication of the message does not lead to acceptance but to disagreement or open hostility. The effective leader learns to use communication in such a positive way that it bolsters the unity of the organization and enhances the quality of human relations. At the same time, it increases productivity toward the achievement of organizational and individual goals.

That is quite a trick, and only the administrator who clearly understands the process of communication can profitably tackle such a task. The focus of this chapter is upon the personal elements in the communications process rather than just the achievement of getting the message through. An understanding and "decoding" of the message is basic, but it is by no means a complete view of interpersonal communications. The executive who is genuinely concerned about the affective (feelings, emotions, attitudes) as well as the cognitive levels of employee understanding will concern himself with the human-relations dimensions of organizational communications. He will learn in short order that the two concepts are virtually inseparable.

J. D. Batten tells about the president of a sizable midwestern company who isolated himself from his people and communicated only through cold, impersonal memo-sending. In an analysis of the company, it was discovered that growth and profit making were very low despite the president's obvious brilliance in business methods. Batten suggests that the man's largest problem was that he "would not recognize the value of human warmth" and was constantly plagued by the problems of interpersonal communication. "Since he was remote and hard to approach, he received only the information he demanded. His subordinates' seeming reluctance to cooperate helped make him increasingly uneasy and suspicious."[1]

Human Needs: Basis for Effective Communication

Because of the administrator's position in the organizational chain of command, he has the greater responsibility toward developing positive human relations through proper use of interpersonal communication. One outstanding psychologist has indicated that a person's usefulness is enhanced in proportion as his linkages with life multiply. The multiple relationships which a leader maintains are dependent upon his ability to keep tabs on all the variable factors which sustain those relationships. This is largely accomplished by means of face-to-face interaction during the working hours.

In the realm of Christian ministry, a proper vertical relationship, with Christ as the head of the church and the Director of all of its leaders, is essential before satisfying and profitable horizontal relationships can be developed and maintained.

UNDERSTANDING PEOPLE'S NEEDS

Part of the problem which many leaders have in developing effective human relations is the very driving nature of their own personalities. The effective leader is generally a person with a high level of personal accomplishment. He has learned ways to get things done, to achieve goals, to obtain results, and to maintain tight rein on his own time. Consequently, he frequently appears to subordinates and colleagues as a cold and calculating person who is quite unapproachable. Such an image immediately puts him at a disadvantage in developing satisfying relationships through interpersonal communications.

The basic needs of people in groups have been explored in the previous chapter. When we apply them to their relationship to the organization, we come up with such things as these:

> Sense of belonging
> Share in planning
> Clear understanding of what is expected
> Genuine responsibility and challenge
> Feeling that progress is being made toward
>   organizational goals
> Intense desire to be kept informed
> Desire for recognition when it is due
> Reasonable degree of security for the future

Although research supports all of these items and more, most good leaders could become aware of human need without the research. The problem with most of us is that we become so entangled with our own problems and our personal, administrative overload, that we fail to recognize and deal with the things we really know are important.

INTERPERSONAL AND INTRAPERSONAL RELATIONS

There are dynamic forces operative within the personality

of an individual worker which have profound effects upon his interactions with other people in his work group. *Intrapersonal* relations describes the phenomena existing within the individual as a feeling, thinking, and expressing person. *Interpersonal* relations focuses on his visible encounters and interaction within the organization.

In one sense, it is correct to say that there is no communication without the interpersonal dimension, since mutuality is a basic ingredient in the communications process. But it is also quite true that the inner factors of personal equilibrium influence the communication process. Meanings are placed upon words as an individual listens to another's communication through his grid of emotional, social, religious, and political prejudices.

Without subscribing to, or even discussing psychoanalysis, we can note that its general theory views individual development as a complex interaction between instinctual processes, the evolving psychic structure, and the changing relations with persons in the environment. So, although interpersonal relations unfold in the present, many psychologists would argue that their meaning, particularly in emotional and symbolic qualities, is distinctly related to the individual's personal history.

One does not have to buy raw Freudianism to nod approvingly toward such an emphasis. If the leader genuinely wants to understand and relate to one of his colleagues, he recognizes that *the interpersonal communications he is attempting to establish are being greatly affected by two sets of intrapersonal factors, his own and those of the other individual.*

STRUCTURING FOR COMMUNICATION

The desirability of breaking up managerial responsibility into smaller units is related to the basic theory of communications and decision-making in administration. Such decentralization enables the administrator to "touch all the bases" in a more comprehensive and yet intensive fashion in his relationships with other persons in his organization. Good administration is multidimensional, and so there are always a number of diverse factors which must of necessity elude the autocratic leader who fancies himself one of the kings of the Gentiles.

One of the axioms of the PERT (Program Evaluation and Review Technique) system states that an event can occur only when all of the activities which lead up to it have been completed, and no succeeding activity may begin until the event is finished. As administrators, we do not have great difficulty applying a rule like this to the process of planning. Sometimes, however, we seem to expect positive communications to just happen, without laying specific groundwork to insure a continuing climate of open communication in the organization.

A Sunday school superintendent, for example, might decide that one of his general purposes for the year is to create a climate of openness and mutually happy interpersonal relations among the departmental superintendents and teachers. One of his objectives for the year might be regular staff meetings which follow a carefully prepared agenda to explore some of the areas of mutual concern. Another objective might be to spend time individually with each of his departmental superintendents individually, attempting to build through those counseling sessions a spirit of rapport and mutual exchange of ideas. As he becomes more specific in delineating goals for the meetings, he will be considering his role as a listener, his response to questions, and his openness in providing thorough information at the staff meetings and in the personal counseling situations.

Some communications experts argue that communication is relative to the centrality of a person in a group. People in the periphery, they suggest, tend to be negative and contribute less to the solution of group problems. Obviously, in a highly centralized bureaucracy there are many more people on the periphery than is the case when decentralization secures an increasing involvement of personnel.

Part of the problem with peripheral people is that they are probably the least informed of the group, and they maintain a constant aura of suspicion regarding the plans and practices of the nuclear control group. So the structure of the organization, even when it is informal, provides for or minimizes the level of interpersonal communications.

UNDERSTANDING COMMUNICATION CHANNELS

An individual's ability to communicate effectively with others depends upon the adequacy of his inputs, the accuracy and appropriateness of the way he treats those inputs, and the techniques he can utilize in composing and delivering a message.

So far, we have only touched upon the sending of the message. If the leader is impressed by the arguments of the symbolic interactionists, he recognizes that words are the basic building-blocks of all conceptual behavior, and he thinks of them as individual stimuli intended to arouse in a receiver the desired intellectual or emotional state. Consequently, words in sentences are the primary tool for the communication of ideas.

A sentence gives form to thoughts and serves as the vehicle for their transmission.* Paragraphs represent the organization of sentences and ideas into larger forms of written communication. But in oral communication, the focus is obviously placed upon words and sentences, both of which can be recognized.

Communication channels in an organization are influenced by internal characteristics and environmental factors. As communications within an organization become stabilized, flows are differentiated, and message contents are affected by their relationships to authority, expertise, friendship, or status.

*See illustration on p. 42.

Think of a church in which a lay member responds with indifference when requested by a fellow lay member to carry out a certain task. The same person jumps immediately to the job if the request comes from the pastor. What has happened is that the content of that communication has been affected by the status of the second sender.

There are a number of different kinds of channels in any kind of institution. What we call formal channels are consciously established to carry messages up and down. A memo is a formal channel, as is a bulletin board, a church newsletter, and announcement time during the Sunday morning service. An informal channel is one which carries the information even though the organization has not specifically planned for it to do so. Mrs. Jones calling Mrs. Smith on Monday morning may very well provide a higher volume of information for either or both of the ladies than they had received during the formal communications the day before.

A channel of communication is *interpersonal* when it is informal and carried out for purposes of information, affection, or mediation of rewards or punishments, and based on personal interests between the communicants.

Sometimes the literature on management speaks about intragroup and intergroup channels. An intragroup channel is a leadership channel, formal or informal, which carries information pertinent to the group's operations. An intergroup channel, on the other hand, is a more formal process designed to convey messages pertinent to the interests of each group within the organization, its relationship with other groups, or its changes. A monthly meeting of the board of Christian education, for example, is concerned largely with intergroup channels of communication, because its responsibility is to coordinate the total educational program of the church.

In *Administrative Communication*, Lee Thayer talks about the uses of communication channels and suggests several guiding principles:

1. The more important, significant, or urgent a message, the more channels should be used.

2. When speed of transmission is the guiding factor, use informal channels. If the message is also an important one, it can be reinforced by also sending it through the slower formal channels.

3. To be authoritative, an official message must pass through formal, organization channels.

4. To be influential, the most advantageous are power and prestige channels, followed by intragroup and intrapersonal channels.

5. Policies are most effectively transmitted through organization channels, but practices are more effectively transmitted through interpersonal channels.

6. A channel which ordinarily "carries" a certain type of message may "carry" other types of messages less effectively.

7. Attitudes are best reached through intragroup, interpersonal, and value channels; knowledge is best reached through the formal and ideological channels.[2]

COMMUNICATION AND MOTIVATION

If mutuality and simultaneity are really crucial factors in the communication process, then no two people can meet without transmitting and reacting to signals of some kind. The communication of A depends upon the response of B, and vice versa. In that kind of communication, the purpose should be to promote appropriate attitudes or action, or possibly to promote understanding without regard to motivation.

This concept is important, because sometimes administrators think only about the motivating role of communications. In other words, they see communication only as a one-way street down which they want to drive their trucks laden with information from the front office. As the trucks dump that information on a waiting populace, individuals and groups within the organization are supposed to respond in accordance with the intent of the executive leadership. When that does not happen, the leaders tend to become hostile, accuse the workers of lack of loyalty, and feel very threatened in their positions of control.

In their helpful book entitled *Interpersonal Communication and the Modern Organization*, Ernest Bormann and his coauthors talk about what they call "a new concept of communication."

> Since 1950 business executives have been peculiarly receptive to a revised concept of communication. For decades the word had conveyed one meaning only—the distribution of information. But in the post war years increasing numbers of thoughtful businessmen began to think of communication as a *two-way process*.
>
> True, management still consisted of getting other people to do things that had to be done. But simply telling others what to do was no longer good enough. Successful managers were those who listened to their employees as frequently as they instructed them. Even if a manager could do nothing immediately in response to an employee's complaints or wishes, he found it highly profitable to learn as directly as possible what his workers were talking and thinking about.[3]

But we are concerned primarily with the development of positive human relations in the Christian organization. Communication is only one of the dimensions of that relationship and environment. Therefore, it may be important to suggest here that whereas communication is still the most strategic factor in group or individual motivation, it ought not to be given over completely to that end. Speaking and listening are tools which the leader can use to build a climate of receptivity and warm, human interaction in the organization. When that organization is also an organism such as the church, the relations of body members one to another may be just as important (some would suggest even more important) then the volume of productivity of the congregation in outreach, community witness, or world evangelization.

When one takes such a view of communication, *clarity* is no longer the only important factor. *Courtesy* now comes in, because the leader recognizes that all of his communication generates feelings, as well as conveys ideas. Although the Scriptures do say, "Great peace have they which love thy law and nothing shall offend them" (Ps 119:165), it is obviously not to the administrator's advantage to push this passage to unwarranted extremes. Every leader must develop his capability to walk alone, if need be, but he must guard against making self-dependency an obsession.

On the positive side, communication and motivation are almost inseparable parts of the leadership function. One of the issues of the Hillsdale College Leadership Letter talks about this phenomenon and likens it to the "two parts of the complete wave of alternating current electricity. We are not always aware of electricity . . . but its presence may produce the results we want, or it may kill us. The same is true of communication and the motivation it does or does not produce."[4]

Churches are talking a great deal today about change, but are spending relatively little time creating the proper atmosphere for change. The questions are virtually rhetorical: how much time do seminary students spend learning the intricacies of administration in order to be agents of motivation in the congregation? What kind of leadership training are we offering lay leaders such as Sunday school superintendents, deacons, and board chairmen? Where are the denominational leaders who have been highly trained in communication and other administrative skills?

AVOIDING COMMUNICATIONS BREAKDOWN

If communications breakdown also means a breakdown in human relations in the organization (and it does), then we must pay careful attention to the problems that we might encounter in the communications process. Experts tell us that the loss in communication can be measured primarily in factors such as foggy detail, distortion of words, retention of emotional concepts, and an attachment to the facts of innate prejudice. In the process, certain central ideas seem to hang on, whereas obscure or misunderstood concepts fade into even greater ambiguity.

The emphasis ought to be clear: *the centrality of the important ideas must be emphasized, and comprehension, not memorization, should be what we look for in the feedback.* Any good college teacher has come to grips with the relationship between *knowing* and *understanding* early in his career. A Sunday school teacher ought not to be as concerned that little Johnny can memorize huge portions of Scripture as she is that he can understand them and feed them back in his own words.

The social setting, or environment, of the communication is also highly important. Dan Lacy suggests that the broadest context of any given communication is the social or cultural environment which we all share. He identifies the kinds of characteristics that the changing nature of a society facing future shock requires in its communications system:

1. That system must be able to record and organize for recall a very much greater body of knowledge than our society has ever before used or indeed now possesses.

2. It must be able to convey to a mass audience information of a high order of complexity such as has before been shared by a rather small elite.

3. It must make possible the continuing education or re-education of adults to a degree never before necessary.

4. To permit the coordination of our increasingly complex society, it must multiply the flow of current information where "news," in quantity, in depth and complexity, and in the number of people to be kept informed.

5. As a protection against the acute danger of an over-

simplification or misrepresentation of problems now per-
ceived almost wholly at second-hand through the media
of communication, the communications system must provide the maximum possible opportunity for the dissemi-
nation of minority, divergent, and critical comment, and
must amplify the individual's opportunity to receive a
diversity of information and points of view that can
challenge and test the accuracy and fulness of the dominant image of those problems.

6. The crisis resulting from the increasingly serious lag between the rate of governmental and institutional change
on the one hand, and the rate of scientific and technologi-
cal change on the other, makes it essential that the communication system do everything possible to encourage,
nourish, and disseminate new ideas and novel approaches
to the solution.

7. In the philosophical disorder of our times, and in view of
the unusual dependence on the media for the derivation
of values and philosophic insights, it is important that
our communications systems be able to afford something
more than the shallow and vacuous re-echoing of the
forms of traditional beliefs, and provide substitutes for
the individual hammering out of new insights.[5]

At this point, it is important to recognize again the John
17 concept of being in the world and yet not of the world.
Because the church is in the world, it finds itself both doing
battle with, and under the compulsion to use the systems of,
the world's culture. Consequently, Paul could write to the
church at Rome and warn its people against the pagan idol-
atry all around them, and yet claim his Roman citizenship
in order to make a desired visit to that city. Perhaps this
is what our Lord meant when He suggested to His disciples
that they must be as "wise as serpents, and harmless as
doves" (Mt 10:16).

Living within the society without becoming a part of the
society has been a difficult task faced by the church since

OPPORTUNITY FOR COMMUNICATION

its earliest days. What is obviously essential is a recognition that biblical separation is neither isolation nor insulation from the culture; therefore the church must recognize and utilize the very principles which Lacy has articulated.

Christian employers' and leaders' openness to the ideas and innovative suggestions of their employees and subordinates ought to characterize the flow of communication in any Christian organization. In an excellent article which appeared in *Personnel Administration* in 1967, John Anderson speaks about the blockades to upward communication. Without going into detail, it might be helpful to at least identify the factors delineated in Anderson's analysis of the problem:

1. It must occur to B that it matters whether he says anything.
2. Once aware that he has significant information, B must choose to pass it on.
3. B must have an opportunity to make his information available to A.

4. If B does speak, A must be able to receive his message.
5. Having listened to and understood B's message, A needs to act on it.[6]

If at any one of these points the communications process goes awry, it can destroy the attempts of a subordinate to communicate with his superior about matters that might be of extreme importance to both.

In the Bormann book mentioned earlier, the authors have delineated, from the many case studies with which they have worked, a profile of the communicating leader. In the profile, they have isolated six characteristics which supposedly mark the man who recognizes that communication with persons in the organization is especially crucial to the survival of his leadership and the ongoing productivity of his institution.

1. *Do not play the role of manipulator.* When a person in an organization constantly uses others to serve his own ends, or perhaps even the ends of the organization, he will soon find himself without a leadership role.

2. *Be willing to pay the price.* It is interesting that in their research, Bormann and his coauthors discovered that almost every person of the work group wanted to be a leader because of the obvious rewards of leadership, but few wanted to be leaders badly enough to assume the enormous responsibility and work load.

3. *Talk up.* The quiet, reticent member of the group is rarely chosen as leader because it does not appear that he has sufficient interest in the group. On the other hand, it is not the quantity of words which makes the difference, but the clarity of the group's objectives and the leader's seeming ability to carry the group toward those objectives.

4. *Do your homework.* "Members who emerge as leaders have sensible, practical ideas and state them clearly."

5. *Give credit to others.* Subordinates are not interested in working toward the glory of their leader, but they are

quite willing to work for their own glory and perhaps even for the glory of the group, assuming they are in complete harmony with its objectives and directions.

6. *Raise the status of other members.* "People who emerge as leaders compliment others when the latter do something for the good of all. . . . In short, they are honestly disinterested in whether they emerge at the top of the pecking order or not—so long as the team does well."[7]

9

The Use and Abuse of Power

POWER HAS COME to be an expected component of the leadership process. Indeed, it has always been commonly considered a part of the total role of leadership in military, business, educational, and religious realms. In a 1970 publication, James Van Fleet urges executives to "control people" by manipulating a few key persons. He argues that it is not necessary "to control the whole human race to be successful. But you can control dozens of people—yes, even hundreds—through just a few key people." In a later, staggering paragraph, his illustration for this style of leadership is Genghis Khan![1] This is the precise attitude of the kings of the Gentiles, who lord it over their subordinates.

Yet, while recognizing the ominous dangers and sinister implications of this kind of autocracy in the Christian organization, we still must recognize that positions of authority and leadership do bring power. So rather than pretending that power is an insignificant factor in the Christian organization, we should talk about its use and abuse, and about the different kinds of power which can be delineated.

THE POWER OF AUTHORITY

The noun form of the Greek word *exousia* is translated in the English text of the King James Version by the word *power* sixty-nine times; *authority* twenty-nine times; *right* two times; and *jurisdiction, liberty,* and *strength,* one time each. It is quite clear that all of the usages of *power* refer to authority or privilege. In Matthew 28, for example, our Lord told His disciples, "All authority is given unto me in heaven and in earth" (v. 18). We read also that our Lord taught as one who had *exousia* (Mt 7:29). And on various occasions His *exousia* was questioned, especially by the Pharisees, who apparently were attempting to protect their own *exousia*. Interestingly enough, the word is translated as *authority* most frequently in the gospels and as *power* most frequently in the epistles. Surely there was some scale of choice, known only to the scribes in 1611, as a rationale for this arrangement.

Although *exousia* appears most frequently with reference to God, it is not uncommonly used of man. So we are not surprised to find Paul suggesting, in Acts 26:12, that he had been sent to Damascus "with authority" to carry out his task of persecution.

It is crucial to understand how the word appears in relation to the church and, more specifically, to leadership and human relations in the church. One common usage is the Romans 13 context, in which the Christian is commanded to be in subjection to the authority of the civic state because the authority of the civic state is a reflection of the *exousia* of God. Another key passage is 1 Corinthians 9:18, where Paul indicates that he does not want to abuse his *exousia* in the gospel. This is similar to a statement in his letter to the church at Thessalonica, in which he argues that he has the authority to request funds for his missionary evangelism. However, he does not want to "pull rank," but rather offer an example for the churches (2 Th 3:9).

Patterson offers a helpful definition when he says:

> Authority thus may be understood as an interpersonal interactional phenomenon in which the one "having authority" influences the behavior of another. The manner of influencing or otherwise affecting behavior (perhaps by raw force of power—a type of authority—or by raw freedom and independence to do just as one pleases—another type of authority) is the particular ingredient in the authority formula that

requires various definitions. The shades of meaning in each particular definition must match up with a type or manner of influencing.[2]

In the context of a church, Patterson argues, "When one is given superior status or 'office' in the authority-power structure, he is then in a legitimate position to exercise personal influence. Then he must prove himself by continually winning the support of 'the subordinates' (or in better Christian terms, 'the members'), whose support is never indefinitely given."[3]

An obviously extreme abuse of power and authority in the church was in the case of Diotrephes, recorded in 3 John. This man loved to have the preeminence in the local assembly, and he carried out his control over the brethren with such total autocracy that he apparently was able to put out of the church anyone who did not act in accordance with his demands. Diotrephes clearly behaved like one of the kings of the Gentiles.

THE POWER OF COMPETITION

Although many professional educators have spoken and written about the negative effects of competition and how it must be eliminated in the educational process, it is still very much with us today. Indeed, it was very much a part of the experience of the early church (Ac 15), simply because it emanates from the basic, human nature of fallen man.

The problem of "competition anxiety" in leadership generally follows one of two patterns—the fear of failure, or the fear of success. The fear of failure is perhaps the most easily recognized and is common, at one time or another, to most people. It can be seen even in children at play and is sometimes reflected by a passive and unwilling attitude. Billy says to his little sister, "I finished dressing before you," and she replies, "I wasn't racing."

As the competition anxiety complex becomes more fixed in adult leadership, it produces levels of self-consciousness and continuing reluctance to become involved in activities for fear of failure. The results are sometimes serious under-achievement and failure to develop a sense of identity. The fear of failure can be ultimately resolved only when the person involved is ready and willing to look at his internal, competitive world, to judge its basis in reality, and either to change the structure or to redesign his self-concept in accordance with realistic and rational standards.

The second pattern of competition and anxiety is the *fear of success,* and its characteristics are virtually the opposite of the other side of the syndrome. Here we are looking at a person who may be extremely outgoing and extroverted. But he develops feelings of guilt while progressively moving up the hierarchy. He generally believes that one can achieve a higher position than he presently has only by displacing or removing someone who is at the next level. Consequently, success brings with it feelings of guilt and desperate attempts to make amends for whatever evidently wrong behavior was involved.

Sometimes a person plagued by fear of success will strive hard in the competitive environment to achieve his goals, seemingly experience the influence of competition, but then stop short before actual achievement. Such behavior succeeds in undoing or avoiding the actual product that may be responsible for his feelings of guilt.

So we seem to be caught on the horns of a dilemma. On the one hand, competition is obviously a very present part of our culture. At the same time, its impact on leadership style is generally negative and not a very high priority item on the spiritual value scale.

Paul suggests that if we go on measuring ourselves by ourselves, we'll never make any progress toward Christian maturity (2 Co 10:12). As we think about the use of authority and power in the Christian organization, our example is the apostle Paul, or perhaps Christ Himself, who was in competition with nothing except the forces of sin. Furthermore, as leaders, it may be our responsibility to control the forces of the situation in which our people live and work.

Like individuals, organizations have values and traditions which influence their behavior. The kind of leaders and workers we want may be determined largely by the way we communicate our values through job descriptions, policy pronouncements, and general public statements. As much as possible, we ought to be playing down the power of competition while, at the same time, uplifting the standard of *koinonia* and mutual burden-bearing.

THE POWER OF POSITION

Research examining the power of political position has developed guidelines for determining the source of power in city politics. Four questions have emerged:

1. How visible is the leadership?
2. How wide is the scope of influence?
3. How cohesive is the power structure, and do decision makers overlap?
4. How legitimate is the power structure?

In most major cities today, the power structure is so complex that there is no clear picture of how decisions are made. Too many varying factors are involved, and, in many decisions, important power-blocs stay out of issues simply to reserve their clout for a future problem which they consider to be more crucial.

Most writers agree, however, that the elected officer represents the most legitimate type of leadership, simply because he has emerged by choice of the group. And in a human-relations view of leadership and administration, the forces inherent in the subordinate group are of extreme importance. (This is not to negate the importance of forces in the individual leader and the situation.)

In thinking through leadership style, the wise executive

recognizes that each subordinate has a set of expectations about how the boss should relate to him. The better a leader understands these factors, the more accurately he can determine what kind of behavior on his part will enable his subordinates to act most effectively. There may be times when an almost autocratic style of leadership is called for because of factors in the subordinates or, perhaps, the situation. On the other hand, there may be kinds of groups with whom the effective leader will pursue an exclusively democratic or even egalitarian leadership style.

In an article in *Harvard Business Review*, Robert Tannenbaum and Warren Schmidt identify certain "essential conditions" in describing groups which can be effectively led through a free, democratic, and human-relations-centered administration:

> If the subordinates have relatively high needs for independence.
>
> If the subordinates have a readiness to assume responsibility for decision-making.
>
> If they have a relatively high tolerance for ambiguity.
>
> If they are interested in the problem and feel that it is important.
>
> If they have the necessary knowledge and experience to deal with the problem.
>
> If they have learned to expect to share in decision-making.[4]

Leaders coming into a new situation must recognize that groups which have been led to expect strong leadership, and then are suddenly confronted with the opportunity to share in decision making and experience wide freedom in the work, tend to become upset and frustrated. The reverse, of course, is also true. A group which has been led by a very democratic leader will resent and perhaps even retaliate against a boss-type autocrat who moves in to take control.

THE POWER OF SELF-REALIZATION

The concept of self-actualization described in chapter seven is not just some idea which has appeared on the drawing boards of social psychologists. An analysis of history seems to indicate that outstanding leaders throughout the ages have had a clear grasp of themselves as persons. Sometimes there was an emphasis on their own importance, even to the point of developing a Napoleonic complex or a neurosis similar to that of Alexander the Great. But there was, apparently, in the lives of most of them, some inherent power of what I am calling *self-realization,* which moved them to achieve beyond the average level.

It is unthinkable that a composer could continue to work after he had become deaf, but Beethoven did just that. Or consider an author like John Milton, who did not allow blindness to interfere with his writing. Or Michelangelo, who wanted to sculpt so badly that he fought against any odds to achieve. Or Winston Churchill, who bounced back from defeat and public humiliation, with an uncanny sense of personal and national destiny, to lead his nation again.

Part of the study of psychocybernetics indicates that thrusting ahead to personal goals and imagining the kind of behavior one would employ in those expected goal situations are sources of power and drive common to many successful leaders. The self-concept of the strong executive is a constantly evolving and changing thing. This sense of growth and self-expectation allows man to search for that unrealized power and to find it.

The difference between a strong leader and a lifetime follower may not be only an overt ability, a keen intelligence, or even drive. Sometimes many ambitious men get nowhere. The secret may lie in the power of self-realization and self-concept. How do I view my life? What do I believe God wants to do with me? What are my values? What are my spiritual gifts? What are my lifetime goals? What does God have to change in my life in order for me to realize those goals?

It is not my intent to make this sound like so much religious humanism. But self-actualization can, indeed, be an analysis of the realization of God-given gifts and capacities exercised through the power of the Holy Spirit and by means of the grace of the heavenly Father. Achievement does not have to be for selfish ends nor does it have to be attained through fleshly efforts.

It seems to me that the apostle Paul is a shining example of the power of self-realization. A man who had achieved far beyond most of his peers, yet perennially dissatisfied with those achievements, he pressed on to higher levels of spiritual growth, wider outreach for the cause of the gospel, and a more significant and lasting impact on the lives of other men (Phil 3:10-14).

THE POWER OF CREATIVITY

The church is scolded from all sides today because of an alleged commitment to traditional systems and an unwillingness to be creative and flexible in a day when new forms and ideas are so desperately needed. Quite obviously, "the church" is people, and when we make (or agree with) this kind of criticism, we are suggesting that somebody, somewhere, is too tradition-bound to allow the church to shed its shackles of ultraconservatism in practice.

But the contemporary church is an organization attempting to maintain equilibrium between two polarized groups. The younger group is pulling toward change, and the older one is pulling against change. It is essential that each share its strengths with the other, and that both recognize the inherent power of creativity and how important it is to an institution and to its leaders.

Creativity seeks new solutions to old problems as well as to new problems. It is not always as rational as it might be, but then, the creative process has never been clearly marked by rationalism. On the other hand, traditionalism is rational. It documents with scientific precision, and generally works only with the known, proven, and measurable. Such a commitment prefers traditional solutions and is suspicious of change.

Creativity also brings with it an aura of flexibility. The institution cannot remain rigid if it allows its leaders to be creative thinkers. When the equilibrium of the organization shakes, the creative pole may attract too strongly, and productive energy can be dissipated down blind alleys. But that is precisely what Albert J. Sullivan has called "The Right to Fail," which he argues is essential if we are going to enjoy the power of the creative process in our institutions.

> The right to fail is of the essence of creativity (just as the prevention of failure is of the essence of conservativism). The creative act must be uninhibited and marked by supreme confidence; There can be no fear of failure—nothing inhibits so fiercely, or shrinks a vision so drastically, or pulls a dream to earth so swiftly, as fear of failure.[5]

If an individual leader is to experience the power of creativity in his own administrative style, he is going to have to live with the right to fail. His church or institution will have to give him the right to fail, not all the time, but at least occasionally. You see, in research and experiment, there really is no such thing as "failure," because it is the *striving* that we measure, not the *reaching*. In creative leadership, one's grasp must always be extended beyond his reach.

Generally speaking, in churches and Christian institutions of education at all levels, the traditionalistic, administrative processes reinforced by the desperate financial crisis of the seventies have all but crushed the right to fail. And with it, a great deal of the potential power of creativity has been crushed.

THE POWER OF QUALITY

One of the great blights on the church in recent years has been its failure to establish strong and adequate systems of quality control. Somehow we have assumed that because our work is being done by volunteer employees, it must therefore be of an inferior quality, and we dare not expect high standards of performance. The result has been an offering to God of shoddy workmanship and programming that does not pass the most elementary tests of adequacy.

The Christian organization should be genuinely interested in quality control. And if it has done its homework, it will soon discover the underlying presupposition of this book: *quality control begins and ends with the people in the organization.* It is not a question of better programs or machinery (as industry has spent millions of dollars to learn), because the performance of the human element in an organization remains beyond the influence of computer processing or statistical techniques. Richard A. Kaimann says it well: "Since it is the worker who builds quality, an attitude of quality mindedness must be developed within him." Kaimann suggests four essential control checks to help a leader who genuinely wants to see quality work among the persons whose performance he supervises.

1. The operator knows what he is *supposed* to be doing;
2. The operator knows what he is *actually* doing;
3. The operator can regulate the process if he fails to meet specifications, and
4. The operator has determination to use every measure to produce conforming products.[6]

Several things are involved here, from a leadership point of view. The first is a *commitment to the power of quality.* No church or school can rid itself of the strangling fingers of mediocrity until it first decides that quality is possible. The second is a *commitment to a Theory-Y view of the work-*

er. What Kaimann calls "quality mindedness" is not an option unless we can really excite the individual Sunday school teacher, youth worker, and board member about the potential of really *good* work. The third is the matter of *training for the task*. And finally, there is the *building in of incentives*, even nonmonetary incentives, to stimulate the kind of interest in the power of quality that must be a part of the worker's life-style.

Here again we are right back to the whole process of a human relations leadership style and the kind of motivation that enters in to achieve quality (see chap. 6).

> The Christian organization which, unwittingly, glosses over deficient performance, or pretends it does not exist, is performing an ultimate disservice.... Perhaps the responsibility for such a situation lies with the management and a lack of comprehension of management principles, Biblically based, which secular organizations seem to be using far more effectively than our Christian organizations.... Managers and executives in Christian organizations should appreciate management as a profession, approach it with respect, and determine to master it.[7]

THE POWER OF THE SPIRIT

In Christian leadership, human ability is a poor substitute for spiritual power. Unfortunately, it is frequently being used in much church ministry today. The Greek word which identifies the supernatural dynamic of the indwelling and filling Holy Spirit is the word *dunamis*. Paul wrote to the Roman Christians, "Now the God of hope fill you with all joy and peace in believing, that ye may abound in hope, through the *power* of the Holy Ghost" (Ro 15:13); and he reminded Timothy that the evidence of the spiritual life was exhibited in *power*, love, and a sound mind (2 Ti 1:7).

But perhaps one of the key passages in the New Testament with respect to the power of the Spirit in ministry is 2 Corinthians 4:7: "But we have this treasure in earthern vessels, that the excellency of the *power* may be of God, and not of us." This dynamic verse, when studied in context, is a clarion call for competence in Christian service and leadership—a competence which makes use of all possible resources and powers which have been discussed in the previous paragraphs. Yet we are told that all of them exist, as it were, "in an earthenware pot," a most unglamorous view of self!

In the final analysis, it is not a matter of spiritual power being paralleled with the power of authority, competition, or position. It is, rather, the continual use of all sources of power for leadership, with each source totally impregnated by this last and all encompassing power, the power of God's Holy Spirit in the life of the believer. It produces a ministry which is not self-initiated but God-given; not self-centered but Christ-centered; and dependent not upon human ability, but upon supernatural power. "Because we have the grace of God to carry on our service for Him, we don't have to quit" (2 Co 4:1, author's paraphrase).

10

Maintaining Institution-Individual Balance

THE HISTORY OF MANAGEMENT SCIENCE might well be told as
a history of the study of role conflict between the individual
and the institution, the man and the organization. Different
terminologies have been employed, down through the years,
to describe this phenomenon and the leadership style of the
administrator. He is called either *nomothetic* (institution-
oriented) or *idiographic* (individual-oriented). Respective-
ly, the styles have been identified as effectiveness or efficiency; producing a product or distributing satisfiers; authority or control; initiating structure or consideration; task
achievement or individual need-meeting.

But it all boils down to one basic question. How can you
keep the organization producing and achieving, while at the
same time keeping its workers satisfied and self-actualized?
The study of man-in-organization relates to an interhistorical
life cycle. Just as an individual must understand his own
personality role, so the supervisor of individuals (the administrator) must understand the roles and responsibilties of
a number of individuals in the work group. He must coordinate their activities in their relationships to each other
and in their individual and collective relationships to the
organization. Just when the leader expects his people to be
consistent, logical, and perfect, they turn out to be incon-
sistent, illogical, and imperfect! At this point, he must decide
whether he can best achieve his administrative goals through

128

doing something about changing people, or through attempting to change the organization (see chaps. 5 and 6).

In the church, the problem is both alleviated and compounded. It is alleviated by the oil of the Holy Spirit, which provides in human relations a supernatural lubricant not available to the secular organization. When properly lubricated, the machinery will work very well toward the achieving of both individual goals and the total purposes of the organization. To this extent, the church is *organism* before it is *organization*. Our problems come when we try to think *only* in terms of organism (the supernatural and invisible union of the body), forgetting that the church is also organization.

If the Christian organization, particularly the church, is operating in accordance with Scripture, it will be the most exquisite demonstration of the principles of human relations administration that the business world has ever seen. The spirit of *koinonia* and unity will literally permeate the body and radiate from it to all of its surrounding environment.

SOURCES OF INSTITUTION-INDIVIDUAL CONFLICT

As with any disease, human relations problems in an organization are best handled by dealing with causes rather than symptoms. The symptoms are quite obvious: dissatisfaction, frequent resignations, friction between subordinates and supervisors, and a general atmosphere of gloom. Achievement in such surroundings is propelled only by a neurotic compulsion to duty rather than the joy of service. Many of the conflicts isolated in the research of secular organizations are also common to Christian organizations.

One of the major causes of conflict is the absence of the positive factors identified in the chapters of this book. When supervisors are not properly relating to subordinates, when outmoded forms of motivation are employed, when power is abused, friction develops and imbalance occurs in institution-individual relationships. But to be more specific, let me delineate some of the sources of difficulty which stem from external factors (environment away from the job) and internal factors (inadequate work situation or poor administrative behavior).

ORGANIZATIONAL EXPECTATIONS VERSUS INDIVIDUAL NEEDS

Strain and conflict arise between the individual and the demands of the institution when expectations and needs are not properly harmonized. The worker begins to feel like a hired hand rather than a member of the team. We do well to remember our Lord's words to his disciples just before the crucifixion: "No longer do I call you slaves; for the slave does not know what his master is doing; but I have called you friends, for all things that I have heard from my Father I have made known to you" (Jn 15:15, NASB). There is no question that the Christian must have unyielding commitment in his service. But that commitment is to the person of Jesus Christ and the universal church, not necessarily to a given local representation of that church.

SELF-ACTUALIZATION VERSUS ASSIGNED ROLES

This is uniquely true in situations in which there are discrepancies between the expectations which an organization holds for a man and the kind of personality development he sees for himself. That is why some pastors are frequently unhappy in new churches. It is also true of some Sunday school teachers who plod on in misery, Sunday after Sunday. And do not forget the Christian college teacher who feels that his talents and training are being "used" by his institution, without proper concern for his own individual development and self-realization.

Many individuals choose to act entirely in accordance with the expectations of their organizations, but such a decision frequently brings unhappiness, and perhaps even incompetence. On the other hand, a choice to follow the nature of one's own personality may well result in job loss.

DIVERSE ROLE EXPECTATIONS

There may be honest differences of opinion among the members of any group as to what an individual is supposed to do. One Christian worker often caught in this dilemma is the director of Christian education. Perhaps he has been called to a church which has never before employed a person of his skill and training. Fifteen different church leaders are expecting him to orient himself to fifteen different aspects of the task. To some he is really a youth director. To others, an administrator of the Sunday school. To still others, a visitation pastor. This multiplicity of role expectation surely contributes to the short terms of service of directors of Christian education during the last fifteen years.

MOBICENTRISM

The mobility of the American family is a continuing problem in the matter of developing solid administrative and leadership styles. The concept of mobicentrism goes a step beyond mere mobility. It suggests, "Movement is not so much a way to get some place or a means to an end as it is an end in itself."[1] Eugene Jennings claims that a person who is mobicentric values action in itself, and is content with extended mobility because it always guarantees change.

Here again, Toffler's *Future Shock* offers insight because it indicates that, for some people, the necessity of change is real, and the absence of change would in itself be a cultural shock! If in Christian service there is a premium on long-term commitment to a ministry, and I believe there is, then mobicentrism is a deterrent to competent Christian service and adequate leadership.

LACK OF SUPPORT AT HOME

Has anyone kept statistics on the number of men who have had to leave the ministry because of deficiency in their family relations? The supporting and encouraging wife is a crucial factor in the hiring and training of executives, as well.

One business management magazine reported a survey of wifely drawbacks. This survey was put together by personnel executives, consulting psychologists, and executive recruiters, who cited these negative characteristics:

Prone to drink too much

Domineering

Poorly informed

Mentally underdeveloped compared to her husband

Resentful toward the company for taking away her husband or forgetting her

Excessively interested in her own career or activities, either social or business, to the detriment of her husband's[2]

With the exception of the first (hopefully), any of these items could be a problem for the Christian leader. Most seminaries have fellowship programs for students' wives, but it is surely safe to say that even the best of such programs falls considerably short of adequately preparing women to hold up their half of the executive syndrome in modern organizations, including the church.

STRESS ON AND OFF THE JOB

There is a reciprocal relationship, positive or negative, between the kind of environment a man experiences at home and the kind of situation in which he works during the day. Research has indicated, for example, that when a worker is surrounded by various different people who depend heavily on him, have power over him, and exert high pressure on him, he typically responds with apathy and withdrawal. He experiences a sense of futility. In such circumstances, his feeling of role conflict is very high, and his job satisfaction is low.[3]

There is probably no way we can alleviate the stress in the modern organization. So it becomes necessary to change the individual in some way, to prepare him to face the pressures and frustrations of executive leadership in today's world. In

Christian ministry, this is primarily the responsibility of the Christian college and seminary.

ORGANIZATION OR INDIVIDUAL: WHO NEEDS TO CHANGE?

In an attempt to refocus the management camera on the worker instead of on the organization, the human relations advocates were led to the assumption that the most satisfying or rewarding organization would be the most efficient. According to some modern writers such as Etzioni, however, both of these approaches have one common deficiency: "Neither saw any basic contradiction or insoluble dilemma in the relationship between the organization's thrust for rationality and the human search for happiness."[4]

While the old, scientific management school narrowed its scope on the formal organization, the human relations movement emphasized the informal organization. What is essential is to recognize the balance between the two. The more recent structuralists attempt to formulate a synthesis theory, relating informal and formal organizations without dwelling on a concern for either the institution or the individual. This broadened outlook takes into consideration:

1. The articulation of both formal and informal elements of the organization
2. The scope of informal groups, and the relations between such groups inside and outside the organization
3. Both lower and higher ranks
4. Both social and material rewards, and the effects on each other
5. The interaction between the organization and its environment
6. Both work and nonwork organizations

Etzioni recognizes the problem, but he does not actually make much of a step toward solving it when he reminds us:

> The ultimate source of the organizational dilemmas

reviewed up to this point is the incomplete matching of the personalities of the participants with their organizational roles. If personalities could be shaped to fit specific organizational roles, or organizational roles to fit specific personalities, many of the pressures to displace goals, much of the need to control performance, and a good part of the alienation would disappear.[5]

Meanwhile, Zaleznik is concerned with changing the individual rather than the organization. He rejects the conclusions of the structuralists, whom he does not consider to have really come to grips with the problem any more effectively than have the exponents of the purely human-relations approach. According to Zaleznik, "The unsolved problem in understanding man in organization centers around the inability of existing theory to grasp the essential dynamics of the individual, and from this understanding to formulate a truly psychosocial theory of organization and leadership."[6]

While agreeing with much of what Zaleznik says, I find myself halting short of reverting to what almost seems to be a revival of the "great man" theory of leadership. Furthermore, I am not nearly so concerned about developing a "psycho-social theory of organization and leadership" as I am about developing a biblical model. It is interesting, of course, that many of the biblical components described in chapter two are also the elements of leadership style which have been discussed most positively in much of the psychosocial literature coming out of the management professions.

Is it possible, then, to be both spiritual and competent? Can the Christian leader be biblical as well as in line with the contemporary thinking of administrative science? It is my contention that he *can* and that administrative science has, in fact, spent millions of dollars to discover that *the biblical pattern of balance between a concern for the individual and the necessity of promoting the goals and productivity of the organization is essentially the best approach to leadership.*

Although in management science there is still a great deal of research with respect to changing either the man or the organization, many of the experts have decided upon the transactional approach between the nomothetic and the idiographic dimensions. In reality, these dimensions exist in constant relationship to and interaction with one another rather than in separate spheres. The individual's values will ultimately determine his behavior, unless he compromises his values for some item of secondary importance, such as salary or position. Therefore the organizational values must somehow be integrated with those of the individual.

The model below was developed by Getzels and Guba and clarifies the kind of difficulties which arise in the institution-individual balance game.[7] The top line indicates institutional plans and roles. The bottom line focuses on the individual. The vertical arrows show the necessity of bringing the conflicts into creative tension to achieve harmony in the organization.

Nomothetic Dimension

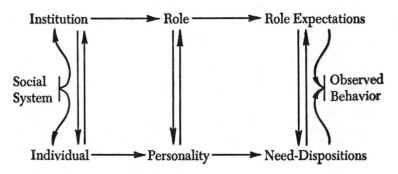

Idiographic Dimension

A Christian position argues that *both* the organization *and* the individual can change, but an emphasis on changing either one to the sacrifice of the other will lead to confusion and turmoil.

SHAPING THE IDIOGRAPHIC CHURCH

It is surely with design that the Scripture speaks frequently of the church as a building and of its members as various blocks of stone in the framework of that building. And just as the architects of a physical building take into account the qualities of the material with which they are working, so must the organizational architects of the church (or other Christian organizations) consider the characteristics of the personnel who make up the structure of their institutions.

The tasks of the human architect are considerably more complex. Qualities of human materials are only partially known, and furthermore, they are notoriously changeable. Some people reject the organization because they feel they have given but have not received. Others pose the opposite problem of taking but wanting to give nothing in return. The result is a sterile organization which, if Christian, becomes a liability rather than an asset to the ongoing ministry of God's work in the world.

Another problem is mobilizing the great amount of human resources the church has and is not using. Industrial science recognizes that the organization can become a deepfreeze in which human resources are stored, rather than an educational experience where the immature become mature; the undeveloped, developed; and the small, increasingly large in outlook and perspective. Douglas McGregor says,

> We have not learned enough about the utilization of talent, about the creation of an organizational climate conducive to human growth. The blunt fact is that we are a long way from realizing the potential represented by the human resources we now recruit into industry. We have much to accomplish with respect to utilization before further improvements and selection will become important.[8]

It is surely possible to substitute the word *church* for *industry* in the above quotation, and to nod to the truth of McGregor's words. The organization is not an end in itself, but rather a means to accomplish the tasks of the worldwide program of Christ.

Church administrators must become aware of the possibility that physical properties can demand such an inappropriate amount of time, talent, and funding that they are no longer an instrument to be used for God's glory, but an object to be hurdled before that glory can be communicated.

A focus on *program* instead of *people* is another albatross in the seventies. In our success-oriented society, we tend to see a large church with a large program as the model, with small churches running along as fast as their tiny, organizational legs can carry them, trying to match the big one. The result is frequently fatigue, disinterest, and rank disillusionment.

It has been said that churches provide a marvelous illustration of the futile attempt to apply raw principles of management to their operations. In the old days, before the pyramid began to crumble, organizational problems were successfully solved by generous applications of things called "techniques of management." But the current stress calls for flexibility rather than rigidity in coping with institutional tensions. Spontaneity and openness are the raw materials out of which creative energy can come to recharge the batteries of Christian organizations in these days of opportunity.

All of the information we can gather about restructuring, administrative forms, leadership styles, and human relations ought to be gathered. Then it should be carefully compared with, and run through, the grid of special revelation. Perhaps what we have left then will be a desirable integration of God's truth revealed in natural forms of order and design, and God's truth in special revelation.

It is *not* a question of baptizing secular research and stuffing it, still damp, into the organizational potholes on the road the church must travel. It is, rather, the application of biblical principles of administration, better understood because we have taken the time to grapple with the secular research.

We are institutions made up of individuals. Our needs are both similar to and diverse from those of secular organizations. But one thing is clear: unless we learn how to be laborers together with each other and with God, our personnel problems will trip us up, just when the world is beginning to see the supernatural dynamic of the body of Christ in the darkness of our contemporary, pagan culture.

Notes

CHAPTER 1

1. "The Frogs and Their King" in *Aesop's Fables.*
2. Robert Tannenbaum and Warren H. Schmidt, "How to Choose a Leadership Pattern," *Harvard Business Review* 36 (March-April 1958): 95.
3. A. B. Bruce, *The Training of the Twelve* (New York: Harper, 1886).

CHAPTER 2

1. Gerhard Kittel, *Theological Dictionary of the New Testament,* S.V. "kubernēsis."
2. Ibid.
3. Kenneth O. Gangel, *Leadership for Church Education.*
4. James M. Lipham, "Leadership and Administration," in *Behavioral Science and Educational Administration,* ed. Daniel E. Griffiths (Chicago: U. of Chicago, 1964), pp. 121-22.
5. Ibid.
6. See chap. six.

CHAPTER 3

1. Unpublished class notes.
2. Francis Schaeffer, *The Church at the End of the Twentieth Century* (Downers Grove, Ill.: Inter-Varsity, 1970), pp. 62-66.
3. Ernest White, "Applying the Priesthood of the Believer to the Life and Work of a Church," *Search* 2, no. 2 (Winter 1972): 13-18.
4. Alan Redpath, *The Royal Route to Heaven* (Grand Rapids: Revell, 1960), p. 152.
5. Schaeffer, p. 56.
6. D. Swan Haworth, *How Church Staff Members Relate* (Nashville, Tenn.: S.S. Brd. of Southern Bapt. Convention, 1969), p. 2.
7. Paul Tournier, *To Understand Each Other* (Richmond, Va.: Knox, 1968), pp. 19-25.
8. Robert Lofton Hudson, *What Makes for Patience?* (Nashville, Tenn.: S.S. Brd. of Southern Bapt. Convention, 1970), p. 7.
9. Walter Liefeld, "The Church: What Did Jesus Intend?" (manuscript).

CHAPTER 4

1. Abraham Zaleznik, *Human Dilemmas of Leadership,* p. 207.
2. F. J. Roethlisberger and William J. Dickson, *Counseling in an Organization* (Boston: Harvard, 1966).
3. Peter Drucker, *The Effective Executive,* p. 71.
4. Ibid., p. 73.
5. Kenneth O. Gangel, *Leadership for Church Education,* p. 296.

6. Robert D. Smith, "Management by Objectives in Church Organizations: Research and Practice," *The Clergy Journal,* November-December 1971, p. 18.
7. Ibid.

CHAPTER 5

1. Chris Argyris, "The Individual and Organization: Some Problems of Mutual Adjustment," in *Educational Administration,* ed. Walter Hack, et al. (Boston: Allyn & Bacon, 1965), pp. 159-82.
2. Ibid., pp. 169-70.
3. Peter Blau, *Bureaucracy in Modern Society* (Chicago: U. of Chicago 1956), p. 14.
4. Peter Drucker, *The Effective Executive,* pp. 23-24.
5. David Riesman, *The Lonely Crowd* (New Haven: Yale U., 1950), p. 112.
6. Warren Bennis, "The Coming Death of Bureaucracy," *Think.*
7. Bill Patterson, "Authority—What It It?" *Christian Bible Teacher,* May 1972, p. 196.
8. Alvin Toffler, *Future Shock* (New York: Random House, 1970), pp. 129, 134.

CHAPTER 6

1. Elton Mayo, *The Human Problems of an Industrial Civilization* (New York: Viking, 1933), p. 180.
2. Ibid., p. 72.
3. Amitai Etzioni, *Modern Organizations,* p. 33.
4. F. J. Roethlisberger and William J. Dickson, *Counseling in an Organization* (Boston: Harvard 1966).
5. B. F. Skinner, *Science and Human Behavior* (New York: Macmillan, 1953), p. 447.
6. Carl R. Rogers, "The Place of the Person in the New World of Behavioral Sciences" (monograph).
7. See chap. eight.
8. Etzioni, p. 75.

CHAPTER 7

1. Mungo Miller, "Understanding Human Behavior and Employee Motivation," *Advanced Management Journal,* April 1968.
2. Milton Rokeach, "Images of the Consumer's Changing Mind on and off Madison Avenue" (Report delivered at the University of Illinois).
3. Ibid.
4. Abraham H. Maslow, *Motivation and Personality* (New York: Harper & Row, 1954), pp. 80-106.
5. Frederick Herzberg, et al. *Job Attitudes: Review of Research and Opinion* (Pittsburgh: Psychological Service of Pittsburgh, 1957); Frederick Herzberg, Bernard Mausner, and Barbara Snyderman, *The Motivation to Work* (New York: Wiley, 1959); Frederick Herzberg, *Work and the Nature of Man* (New York: World, 1966).
6. Herzberg, *Work and the Nature of Man.*
7. George Strauss and Leonard R. Sayles, *Personnel: The Human Problems of Management,* p. 137.
8. Abraham Zaleznik, *Human Dilemmas,* pp. 5-9.
9. David Moment and Abraham Zaleznik, *Casebook on Interpersonal Behavior in Organizations* (New York: Wiley, 1964), p. 2.

10. Douglas McGregor, "Theory X: The Traditional View of Direction and Control," in *An Introduction to School Administration*, p. 175.
11. Ibid., pp. 167-68.
12. Ibid., p. 176.
13. Robert E. Coleman, *The Master Plan of Evangelism* (Westwood, N.J.: Revell, 1964).

CHAPTER 8

1. J. D. Batten, *Tough-minded Management* (New York: AMA, 1963), p. 141.
2. Lee O. Thayer, *Administrative Communication* (Homewood, Ill.: Irwin, 1961), pp. 254-55.
3. Ernest Bormann et al., *Interpersonal Communication and the Modern Organization*, p. 175.
4. "For Those Who Must Lead . . . ," *The Hillsdale College Leadership Letter* 9, no. 9: 1.
5. Dan Lacy, *Freedom in Communications* (Urbana, Ill.: U. of Ill., 1965), pp. 23-24.
6. John Anderson, "What's Blocking Upward Communication?" *Personnel Administration*, January-February 1968.
7. Bormann, pp. 75-77.

CHAPTER 9

1. James K. Van Fleet, *Power with People* (West Nyack, N.Y.: Parker, 1970), p. 18.
2. Bill Patterson, "Authority—What Is It?", *Christian Bible Teacher*, May 1972, p. 195.
3. Ibid., p. 197.
4. Robert Tannenbaum and Warren Schmidt, "Choosing a Leadership Pattern," *Harvard Business Review* 36 (March-April 1958): 99.
5. Albert J. Sullivan, "The Right to Fail," *Journal of Higher Education* 34, no. 4 (April 1963), p. 191
6. Richard A. Kaimann, "Quality Control: The Man Not the Machine," *Management of Personnel Quarterly*, Winter 1968, pp. 8-12.
7. Ted W. Engstrom and R. Alec MacKenzie, *Managing Your Time*, p. 108.

CHAPTER 10

1. Eugene Jennings, "Mobicentric Man," *Psychology Today*, July 1970.
2. "Executive Wives: A Factor in Hiring," *Printers Ink*, August 3, 1962, pp. 19-25.
3. "Stress: From 9 to 5," *Psychology Today*, September 1969, pp. 34-38.
4. Amitai Etzioni, *Modern Organizations*, p. 75.
5. Ibid.
6. Abraham Zaleznik, *Human Dilemmas of Leadership*.
7. J. W. Getzels and E. G. Guba, "Social Behavior and the Administrative Process," *The School Review* 65 (Winter 1957): 423-41.
8. Douglas McGregor, *The Human Side of Enterprise*, p. vi.

Bibliography

Barnard, Chester. *The Functions of the Executive.* Cambridge, Mass.: Harvard U., 1968.

Bell, A. Donald. *How to Get Along with People in the Church.* Grand Rapids: Zondervan, 1960.

Bennis, Warren G. *Changing Organizations.* New York: McGraw-Hill, 1966.

Bormann, Ernest G., et al. *Interpersonal Communication in the Modern Organization.* Englewood Cliffs, N.J.: Prentice-Hall, 1969.

Brown, J. A. C. *The Social Psychology of Industry.* Baltimore: Penguin, 1954.

Browne, C. G., and Cohn, Thomas S., eds. *The Study of Leadership.* Danville, Ill.: Interstate, 1958.

Campbell, Roald F. et al. *The Organization and Control of American Schools.* Columbus, Ohio: Merrill, 1965.

Cartwright, Dorwin, and Zander, Alvin, eds. *Group Dynamics: Research and Theory.* New York: Harper & Row, 1953.

Drucker, Peter F. *Managing for Results.* New York: Harper & Row, 1964.

———. *The Effective Executive.* New York: Harper & Row, 1966.

Engstrom, Ted W., and McKenzie, R. Alec. *Managing Your Time.* Grand Rapids: Zondervan, 1967.

Etzioni, Amitai. *Modern Organizations.* Englewood Cliffs, N.J.: Prentice-Hall, 1964.

Ford, George L. *Manual on Management for Christian Workers.* Grand Rapids: Zondervan, 1964.

Gangel, Kenneth O. *Leadership for Church Education.* Chicago: Moody, 1970.

———. *So You Want to Be a Leader!* Harrisburg, Pa.: Christian Pubns., 1973.

Giffin, Kim, and Patton, Bobby R. *Fundamentals of Interpersonal Communication.* New York: Harper & Row, 1971.

Griffiths, Daniel E., ed. *Behavioral Science and Educational Administration.* Chicago: Nat. Soc. for Study of Ed., 1964.

Hack, Walter G., et al., eds. *Educational Administration: Selected Readings.* Boston: Allyn & Bacon, 1965.

Halpin, Andrew W. *Theory and Research in Administration.* New York: Macmillan, 1966.

Herzberg, Frederick. *Work and the Nature of Man.* Cleveland: World, 1966.

Jackson, B. F., Jr., ed. *Communication-Learning for Churchmen.* New York: Abingdon, 1968.

Judy, Marvin T. *The Multiple Staff Ministry.* New York: Abingdon, 1969.

Kilinski, Kenneth K., and Wofford, Jerry C. *Organization and Leadership in the Local Church.* Grand Rapids: Zondervan, 1973.

Lacy, Dan. *Freedom and Communications.* Urban: U. of Ill., 1965.

Larson, Bruce, and Osborne, Ralph. *The Emerging Church.* Waco, Tex.: Word, 1970.

Mager, Robert F., and Pipe, Peter. *Analyzing Performance Problems.* Belmont, Calif.: Fearon, 1970.

McGregor, Douglas. *The Human Side of Enterprise.* New York: McGraw Hill, 1960.

Netzer, Lanore A., et al., eds. *Interdisciplinary Foundations of Supervision.* Boston: Allyn & Bacon, 1970.

Nolte, M. Chester, ed. *An Introduction to School Administration.* New York: Macmillan, 1966.

Richards, Lawrence O. *A New Face for the Church.* Grand Rapids: Zondervan, 1970.

Savage, William W. *Interpersonal and Group Relations in Educational Administration.* Glenview, Ill.: Scott Foresman, 1968.

Shepherd, Clovis R. *Small Groups.* San Francisco: Chandler, 1964.

Stedman, Ray. *Body Life.* Glendale, Calif.: Regal, 1972.

Strauss, George, and Sayles, Leanord R. *Personnel: The Human Problems of Management.* Englewood Cliffs, N.J.: Prentice-Hall, 1960.

Toffler, Alvin, *Future Shock.* New York: Random House, 1970.

Wolff, Richard. *Man at the Top.* Wheaton, Ill.: Tyndale, 1969.

Worley, Robert C. *Change in the Church: A Source of Hope.* Philadelphia: Westminster, 1971.

Zaleznik, Abraham. *Human Dilemmas of Leadership.* New York: Harper & Row, 1966.